What's New in SQL Server 2012

Unleash the new features of SQL Server 2012

Rachel Clements

Jon Reade

BIRMINGHAM - MUMBAI

What's New in SQL Server 2012

Copyright © 2012 Packt Publishing

All rights reserved. No part of this book may be reproduced, stored in a retrieval system, or transmitted in any form or by any means, without the prior written permission of the publisher, except in the case of brief quotations embedded in critical articles or reviews.

Every effort has been made in the preparation of this book to ensure the accuracy of the information presented. However, the information contained in this book is sold without warranty, either express or implied. Neither the authors, nor Packt Publishing, and its dealers and distributors will be held liable for any damages caused or alleged to be caused directly or indirectly by this book.

Packt Publishing has endeavored to provide trademark information about all of the companies and products mentioned in this book by the appropriate use of capitals. However, Packt Publishing cannot guarantee the accuracy of this information.

First published: October 2012

Production Reference: 1051012

Published by Packt Publishing Ltd.
Livery Place
35 Livery Street
Birmingham B3 2PB, UK.

ISBN 978-1-84968-734-8

www.packtpub.com

Cover Image by Jackson Myers (jax@rice.edu)

Credits

Authors
Rachel Clements
Jon Reade

Reviewers
Phil Brammer
Raunak Jhawar

Acquisition Editor
Dilip Venkatesh

Lead Technical Editor
Unnati Shah

Technical Editors
Manasi Poonthotham
Zinal Shah

Copy Editors
Insiya Morbiwala
Alfida Paiva
Laxmi Subramanian

Project Coordinator
Vishal Bodwani

Proofreader
Aaron Nash

Indexer
Rekha Nair

Graphics
Aditi Gajjar

Production Coordinator
Nitesh Thakur

Cover Work
Nitesh Thakur

About the Authors

Rachel Clements has worked as a software and database developer for over 15 years across a wide variety of private industries. She is currently a SQL Server BI Developer for an international power tools company in the UK. Her role encompasses all aspects of the BI stack, along with key database administration tasks.

After graduating from Solent University with a degree in Journalism, she began her career in London writing for The Times technology supplement, before becoming a full-time developer. She now specializes in SQL Server and business intelligence, writes articles for SQL Server Club (www.sqlserverclub.com), and tweets at @RachelClements.

As an active member of the technical community, she organizes the Bristol user group SQL Server Club (www.sqlserverclub.co.uk) and is a member of the Developer! Developer! Developer! South West team (www.dddsouthwest.com). Furthermore, Rachel is a regular volunteer at Europe's largest SQL Server conference, SQLBits.

Acknowledgment

Writing a book was a dream I had since I first began using a pen. Little did I know as a young child learning to write, that my first book would be a technical one! The experience of writing this book has been like none other, and what a memorable one at that. I had no idea just how much work or how many people would be involved: it really is a team effort!

There are many committed people at Packt Publishing who have been instrumental in bringing this book to life. I would like to thank Sonali Tharwani, Vishal Bodwani, Dilip Ventakesh, Unnati Shah, and Zinal Shah, for their crucial roles in organizing and supporting us. I must say a huge thank you to Phil Brammer and Raunak Jhawar for reviewing the book from start to finish and their fantastic suggestions to enhance the quality and usefulness of the content. Additionally, I would like to thank Allan Mitchell for his strong contribution and honest feedback. I am sure there are further people at Packt Publishing who were involved that I did not come into contact with: thank you everyone for the part you played in the delivery of this book!

I am further indebted to Li Li and Alison Coughtrie for their invaluable contribution. Thank you both for giving up your free time to review the book and provide such positive feedback. I am also grateful for the contribution Simon Robinson made to the section on Hadoop. Your knowledge and input has vastly improved this book and I will be delighted to buy you a beer to say thank you!

My gratitude extends to my dear father Colin Clements. Thank you for reading the book and making so many vital suggestions. It means so much to me that you have been a part of it.

My biggest thanks, of course, go to Jon for inviting me to co-author this book. To deliver a book even of this size is no easy task and at times it was tough working all those evenings and weekends. However, this has been such a rewarding experience and I am proud of our first attempt at book writing. Thank you for believing in me enough to give me this opportunity. Working with you is always a pleasure: I learned so much and had tremendous fun!

Jon Reade has worked in the UK and Europe as a database professional in the finance and telecommunication sectors for 16 years. He is currently a SQL Server consultant in the finance industry, based in the UK.

He began his career as a Systems Programmer for IBM, methodically testing and breaking mainframe DB2 database security systems. He graduated with a degree in Computer Science from Aston University in Birmingham before moving on to various database development roles.

He has extensive experience of SQL Server from 6.0 to 2012, in development, operational, production, and managerial roles. He is interested in business intelligence and big data, and the use of data mining to extract useful business knowledge from transactional systems. He holds MCITP and MCTS certifications for SQL Server 2008 and is a recent MSc Business Intelligence graduate from the University of Dundee, Scotland.

He is also a part-time SQL Server instructor for a global training company and the co-founder of the SQL Server Club website (www.sqlserverclub.com) and user group. He tweets (@JonReade), speaks at SQL Server events (SQLBits, DDD South West and SQL Server Club), and has written for Packt Publishing and SQL Server Central.

Acknowledgment

This, my first book, is dedicated to Steve Potts, an extraordinary teacher. He willingly gave up his lunchtimes and endless extra hours teaching an intense, hyperactive, and very inquisitive eleven-year old how to solder together computers and write 6502 assembly language. Amazingly, I can still do both! If you are reading this Steve, a huge "thank you"—it was time well invested. You kindled an interest for life that turned into a career that has taken me to some fascinating places no one could have imagined back then.

In chronological order, I would like to thank Dilip Ventakesh at Packt Publishing, who first approached me with the idea for this book back in 2011. Likewise to Professor Mark Whitehorn, Chair of Analytics at the University of Dundee in Scotland, who not only encouraged me in this endeavor, but spent his valuable time taking me through an impromptu telephone crash course on authoring.

Equal thanks go to our patient reviewers at Packt Publishing, especially Sonali Tharwani, who together with our external reviewers, Phil Brammer (@PhilBrammer) and Raunak Jhawar, reviewed every chapter of this book. I would also like to thank Allan Mitchell, who gave us very useful and detailed feedback on the BI stack chapters.

An extra special thanks must be extended to Simon Robinson, a good friend and colleague, and Senior Software Engineer at Nokia. I had the pleasure of working closely with Simon for three years, and know him as a highly competent database developer and DBA. He not only reviewed the Hadoop chapter for us, but also added valuable extra content born out of his greater experience with Hadoop in a production environment. Thanks Simon!

My final reviewer thanks also go to two fellow database professionals, who are also good friends, for their dedication to this title. Alison Coughtrie, Data Warehouse Architect at the University of Dundee in Scotland, and Lynlee Moon (Li Li), EMEA DBA Manager at NewEdge in London, who have both done great jobs at very short notice turning around their reviews. A personal "thank you" from me to both of you.

Of course my final thanks must go to my co-author and SQL Server BI Developer, Rachel. Over ten months, we have spent every weekend and countless evenings researching, writing, and rewriting this book as the shifting sands of a brand new and very large SQL Server release have moved beneath our feet. Your journalistic training, writing discipline, attention to detail, and enthusiasm have all made this a better book than I could have written by myself, and it has been good fun and a pleasure writing it with you. Somehow, and thankfully, your good sense of humor has remained intact! A big thank you for being a great co-author who has truly shared an immense effort.

When do you want to start writing the next one?

About the Reviewers

Phil Brammer, a sixth year Microsoft MVP in SQL Server and a Microsoft Certified Solutions Expert, has over 12 years' data management experience in various technologies from reporting through ETL to database administration. A full-time DBA managing over 120 database instances in the health-care insurance industry, he also works with SQL Server Integration Services and continues to play an active role in the SQL Server community via online resources as well as his technical blog site, SSISTalk.com. He has contributed to SQL Saturdays, SQL PASS Summits, and the first volume of the SQL Server MVP Deep Dives book. Phil is an avid golfer and loves spending time with his wife and two children.

Raunak Jhawar is an engineering graduate in Computer Science from the University of Pune, India. He works as a full time SQL developer specializing in Microsoft Business Intelligence. In his spare time, he enjoys reading and driving his car.

He can be reached at his e-mail raunak.jhawar@gmail.com and his Twitter handle is @raunakjhawar.

www.PacktPub.com

Support files, eBooks, discount offers and more

You might want to visit www.PacktPub.com for support files and downloads related to your book.

Did you know that Packt offers eBook versions of every book published, with PDF and ePub files available? You can upgrade to the eBook version at www.PacktPub.com and as a print book customer, you are entitled to a discount on the eBook copy. Get in touch with us at service@packtpub.com for more details.

At www.PacktPub.com, you can also read a collection of free technical articles, sign up for a range of free newsletters and receive exclusive discounts and offers on Packt books and eBooks.

http://PacktLib.PacktPub.com

Do you need instant solutions to your IT questions? PacktLib is Packt's online digital book library. Here, you can access, read and search across Packt's entire library of books.

Why Subscribe?

- Fully searchable across every book published by Packt
- Copy and paste, print and bookmark content
- On demand and accessible via web browser

Free Access for Packt account holders

If you have an account with Packt at www.PacktPub.com, you can use this to access PacktLib today and view nine entirely free books. Simply use your login credentials for immediate access.

Instant Updates on New Packt Books

Get notified! Find out when new books are published by following @PacktEnterprise on Twitter, or the *Packt Enterprise* Facebook page.

Table of Contents

Preface

Microsoft SQL Server has been a part of the enterprise database landscape since SQL Server 7 arrived in 1998, and has evolved into the relational and BI platform of choice by businesses around the globe. The performance and full feature set of SQL Server has been widely recognized by the business community and it is viewed as a powerful weapon in their database and business intelligence arsenal. SQL Server brings numerous benefits, and central to their successful implementation, is a thorough understanding of the technology, both current and new.

We have written the book that we, as working DBAs and developers, would want to read. This is the book we always wanted to buy, but could never find in the bookstore. When Packt Publishing initially approached us with the idea of a SQL Server 2012 book, we discussed the issue of "What's New…" books always being padded out with too much old stuff we already knew. They agreed to let us write this - a SQL Server book that contains the new features, and only the new features, in SQL Server 2012.

This book was written with the deliberate intent of giving you a competitive advantage by helping you quickly learn and understand the new features of SQL Server 2012. Most readers will already have an established knowledge of SQL Server and will want to update their 2008/2008 R2 knowledge swiftly, and with the least pain. We understand the importance of keeping up-to-date with current technologies, both in terms of your career development, and implementing new features to give your employer a competitive advantage.

In the modern time-pressured world, it can be difficult to find adequate time to learn new skills. We have done our very best to provide you with a concise and useful reference for SQL Server 2012, and we hope you find this book worthy of a permanent position on your desk.

What this book covers

Chapter 1, Installing SQL Server 2012, shows you the differences between the new editions of SQL Server 2012. A step-by-step guide will walk you through installing the core database engine and advanced options. You will receive advice along the way, to help you maximize the performance of your installation.

Chapter 2, SQL Server Administration, will make you familiar with the new look SQL Server Management Studio, and then you will discover spatial indexes and columnstore indexes. You will also delve into contained databases and Master Data Services, and learn about the new dynamic management views.

Chapter 3, Transact SQL, teaches you how to write queries using the new string and datetime functions inside real world examples. You will explore the error handling clauses, and see how the new FileTable table type builds on existing filestream functionality. You will be formally introduced to SQL Server Data Tools, your new home for SQL development, and learn how to use the new analytical functions.

Chapter 4, Analysis Services, covers the three business intelligence semantic models, the differences between them, and also how to create them. You will discover how to utilize resource usage reporting, geek out with extended events, and learn how to work around the string store constraint, using scalable string storage.

Chapter 5, Reporting Services, shows you which features have been deprecated in SQL Server Reporting Services 2012. You will learn how to use the new Excel and Word Renderers, and how to set up Data Alerts.

Chapter 6, Integration Services, introduces you to the new SSIS catalog, the SSIS Admin security role, and how to upgrade from SQL Server 2005 and 2008. You will learn about shared connection managers, deployment models and package editor enhancements. Furthermore you will look at data taps and Change Data Capture.

Chapter 7, Data Quality Services, explains why you would want to use Data Quality Services, and how to install and configure it. You will learn how to create a data quality project and cleanse data using real world examples. Furthermore, you will gain knowledge DQS security issues.

Chapter 8, AlwaysOn, will investigate AlwaysOn Availability Groups and their restrictions, and will teach you how to create an availability group in your own environment. You will learn about the advantages of AlwaysOn Availability Groups compared to other high availability solutions.

Chapter 9, Distributed Replay, will make you familiar with the new terminology and the components that constitute Distributed Replay. A hands-on example will help you understand how to install and configure it. You will capture a trace, preprocess it, replay it and monitor its progress, and then cancel it.

Chapter 10, Big Data and the Cloud, introduces you to SQL Azure and how to set up and migrate to a SQL Azure database. You will learn about big data platforms, discover the Hive database and be introduced to the Sqoop connector. Finally, you will learn about Microsoft's up-and-coming Hadoop release for Windows and SQL Server.

What you need for this book

You need the following:

- Windows Server 2008 SP2, Windows Server 2008 R2 SP1, Windows Server 2012, or Windows 7 SP1.

- SQL Server 2012 Enterprise Edition (Evaluation Edition or Developer Edition will do).

- A link to download SQL Server 2012 Evaluation Edition is provided in Chapter 1.

Who this book is for

This concise reference is for database administrators, SQL Server developers and BI professionals. Anyone who is familiar with SQL Server 2008 R2 and needs to make the jump to the latest version with the shortest learning curve will find this book useful.

Conventions

In this book, you will find a number of styles of text that distinguish between different kinds of information. Here are some examples of these styles, and an explanation of their meaning.

Code words in text are shown as follows: "We can include other contexts through the use of the `include` directive."

A block of code is set as follows:

```
CREATE TABLE #Customer
(
   FirstName varchar(30) NOT NULL,
   MiddleName varchar(30) NULL,
   LastName varchar(30) NOT NULL
)
```

When we wish to draw your attention to a particular part of a code block, the relevant lines or items are set in bold:

```
[default]
exten => s,1,Dial(Zap/1|30)
exten => s,2,Voicemail(u100)
exten => s,102,Voicemail(b100)
exten => i,1,Voicemail(s0)
```

Any command-line input or output is written as follows:

 # cp /usr/src/asterisk-addons/configs/cdr_mysql.conf.sample
/etc/asterisk/cdr_mysql.conf

New terms and **important words** are shown in bold. Words that you see on the screen, in menus or dialog boxes for example, appear in the text like this: " The **Distributed Replay Controller** server reads transactions from the intermediate file".

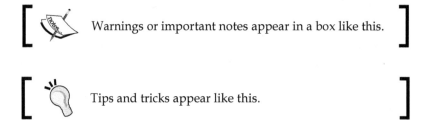

Warnings or important notes appear in a box like this.

Tips and tricks appear like this.

Reader feedback

Feedback from our readers is always welcome. Let us know what you think about this book—what you liked or may have disliked. Reader feedback is important for us to develop titles that you really get the most out of.

To send us general feedback, simply send an e-mail to `feedback@packtpub.com`, and mention the book title via the subject of your message.

If there is a topic that you have expertise in and you are interested in either writing or contributing to a book, see our author guide on `www.packtpub.com/authors`.

Customer support

Now that you are the proud owner of a Packt book, we have a number of things to help you to get the most from your purchase.

Downloading the example code

You can download the example code files for all Packt books you have purchased from your account at `http://www.PacktPub.com`. If you purchased this book elsewhere, you can visit `http://www.PacktPub.com/support` and register to have the files e-mailed directly to you.

Errata

Although we have taken every care to ensure the accuracy of our content, mistakes do happen. If you find a mistake in one of our books—maybe a mistake in the text or the code—we would be grateful if you would report this to us. By doing so, you can save other readers from frustration and help us improve subsequent versions of this book. If you find any errata, please report them by visiting `http://www.packtpub.com/support`, selecting your book, clicking on the **errata submission form** link, and entering the details of your errata. Once your errata are verified, your submission will be accepted and the errata will be uploaded on our website, or added to any list of existing errata, under the Errata section of that title. Any existing errata can be viewed by selecting your title from `http://www.packtpub.com/support`.

Piracy

Piracy of copyright material on the Internet is an ongoing problem across all media. At Packt, we take the protection of our copyright and licenses very seriously. If you come across any illegal copies of our works, in any form, on the Internet, please provide us with the location address or website name immediately so that we can pursue a remedy.

Please contact us at copyright@packtpub.com with a link to the suspected pirated material.

We appreciate your help in protecting our authors, and our ability to bring you valuable content.

Questions

You can contact us at questions@packtpub.com if you are having a problem with any aspect of the book, and we will do our best to address it.

1
Installing SQL Server 2012

When Microsoft releases a major new version of a software product that is as big as SQL Server, it is an exciting time. They are on a schedule of one major release every four years and every release is increasingly more remarkable than the last.

Between us, the authors, we have covered a variety of development and administration roles spanning several decades. Over this time we have taken much delight in watching SQL Server grow stronger, gain more market share, take on new features, and even fix some critical issues too. We started working with SQL Server 6.5 way back in the 1990s and it has been a fascinating journey, arriving here in 2012 with new features that we could hardly have envisaged all those years ago.

Whether you are a database administrator or developer, business intelligence specialist, or .NET developer using SQL Server at the backend of your applications, there are lots of new features in this release to help you in your day-to-day work. There is a lot to discover in SQL Server 2012 and we have brought to you what we feel are the best and most useful of all the new features. Throughout this book there are hints and tips gained over our many years of experience, included to help you get the most out of SQL Server.

In this chapter, we will look at the new editions of SQL Server 2012. In addition to the usual suspects, we now have Cloud and Business Intelligence editions. We will also look at obtaining SQL Server and pre-installation advice as well as what a typical installation looks like. So without further ado, let's jump in.

SQL Server 2012 Editions

Microsoft has changed the available editions with the launch of SQL Server 2012. A new Business Intelligence Edition now joins Standard and Enterprise; however if you are looking for Datacenter, Workgroup, or Web Editions, you will not find them as Microsoft has dropped them. Developer and Express Editions are still very much alive.

Your purchase of SQL Server 2012 is very likely to be budget-driven. Microsoft has two licensing options, based either on computing power (core based), or if you are buying Standard or Business Intelligence editions, on the number of devices or users (Client Access License or CAL). If you are buying new hardware to support SQL Server, then this may leave you with no option but to go for a cheaper version than Enterprise if the bulk of your budget has already been spent on storage and memory. Microsoft's Assessment and Planning Toolkit is a useful tool for license planning and utilization and can be found on the TechNet site at `http://www.microsoft.com/sam/en/us/map.aspx`.

 Take a look at the requirements on the Microsoft site for the most up-to-date information about supported hardware: `http://www.microsoft.com/sqlserver`.

After any budget limitations have been addressed, you will need to consider the workload that your SQL Server will undertake. Performance is important, so if you have many users hitting the server in parallel or a heavy amount of processing, then Standard Edition may not be sufficient.

Let us think about the underlying hardware. Disk speed and memory are where you want to focus your attention to achieve the best performance from your SQL Server. Always make sure you have enough disks and RAM.

Ideally you do not want to put all your disk I/O onto a single spindle, so splitting the load is always a good idea. You will want to put your database files (`.mdf`) on separate drives to your log (`.ldf`) files for a very good reason. In a typical Online Transactional Processing (OLTP) system, SQL Server will access your data files in a random manner as the disk is written to, and read from. For the most part the log file is written to sequentially, so the disk head moves more uniformly. Any interruption to this uniform disk head movement, such as random reads or writes to a data file, will incur latency delays.

 If you are installing Virtual Machines (VMs) then the same rules apply. If your logical drives map onto a single image then all your I/O will go through the same drive. Be careful to split these off too.

What about solid state? If you are lucky enough to be using solid state disks (SSDs), then it is the same principle. Install your data files on your SSDs and your log files on the usual non solid state disks. If you are writing sequentially to a log file then there is less performance gain to be made by using an SSD, so save these for your tempdb and data file operations. However if you have multiple log files on the same drive, then advantages may be gained by using SSDs. You are advised to read about how best to provide resilience to your SSDs as this differs from vendor to vendor. Suffice to say it is best NOT to assume that traditional RAID1/RAID5 arrays are the way to go because of the very different operational characteristics of SSD devices. If you are interested in finding out more about SQL Server and SSDs, have a look at the performance tests on SQL Server MVP Tony Rogerson's blog at `http://sqlblogcasts.com/blogs/tonyrogerson`.

So let's take a look at the new line-up:

Enterprise Edition

The Enterprise Edition continues to be the major version, delivering all services and all features. If your production systems require top-end mission critical features such as asynchronous mirroring or automatic page repair, then it is unlikely you will consider any other version. There are a couple of major new features in SQL Server 2012 which we are really excited about.

First is the addition of **AlwaysOn Availability Groups**. If you are currently using database mirroring you will want to explore availability groups. An availability group allows you to group related databases together, so they failover as a group. Unlike mirroring, you do not have to choose between either synchronous or asynchronous replicas, you can have a mix of both. See *Chapter 8, AlwaysOn*, for more details.

Second up is the introduction of **columnstore indexes**. Are you developing a data warehouse? Then you will be interested in these new indexes for sure. A columnstore index lives up to its name, in that all data from one column, rather than one row, is stored on the same data page or pages. Star schema queries using columnstore indexes execute faster than normal indexes as most values are retrieved from a single page, rather than from rows spanning multiple pages.

The Enterprise Edition boasts advanced security features, such as database-level audit and Transparent Data Encryption. It also includes previous Enterprise Edition only features such as online index rebuilds, data compression, and table partitioning, none of which are available in Standard or BI Editions.

Standard Edition

Standard Edition supports up to 16 cores and along with OLTP capabilities, it offers some basic BI features. It doesn't have all of the new features introduced in Enterprise Edition, so it would be wise to check the feature comparison chart on Microsoft's website before making your purchasing decision at `http://www.microsoft.com/sqlserver`.

There is less emphasis on BI and advanced security in Standard Edition but, with a lower price tag, it may be appropriate for some of your less-critical operations. You will not benefit from AlwaysOn, or from Power View or PowerPivot, or the data management services Data Quality Services (DQS) and Master Data Services (MDS), which are all more data warehouse and BI-specific, but it will very reliably run your OLTP databases.

Business Intelligence Edition

If you do not want the whole feature set that Enterprise Edition offers, but need to do some business intelligence gathering and processing, then this new edition may do the job. The database engine supports up to 16 cores, while SSRS and SSAS can use the maximum that your OS supports.

We were both surprised by the omission of columnstore indexes in this version as these new indexes will bring performance gains to any data warehouse. However, if you decide on Business Intelligence Edition, you will benefit from most of the other BI features available in Enterprise Edition including Power View, PowerPivot for SharePoint Server, Data Quality Services (DQS) and Master Data Services (MDS).

We will take a quick look at the new features in MDS in *Chapter 2, SQL Server Administration*, and an in-depth look at DQS in *Chapter 7, Data Quality Services*. Power View and PowerPivot are beyond the scope of this book.

Licensing in the Cloud

If you are running cloud-based SQL Servers then you will be pleased to hear that Microsoft has included cloud and VM servers in their 2012 licensing model. This should give you enough flexibility to pay for only what you need and a number of options are included. Please see the Microsoft licensing datasheet at `http://www.microsoft.com/sqlserver/en/us/get-sql-server/licensing.aspx` for more information.

Developer Edition

This is the version you will install in your development and test environments. Identical to Enterprise Edition, it has everything you need to replicate your production environment. The only limitation is that it is not used as a production server. Check out the prices on Amazon; at the time of writing, SQL Server 2012 Developer Edition retails at around $60.

 Whichever editions you purchase for your production environment, always go with the Developer Edition in your development and test environments. This will save you lots of money without compromising on features.

Express Edition

This free and lightweight edition, though not heavy-duty enough to be installed in your server room, is useful for small or mobile applications and worthy of a mention. There are add-on tools to manage the Express Edition, which are perfect for developers needing the bare minimum of requirements.

Consider your needs carefully and check the full list of features on the Microsoft comparison matrix before you make your purchase, at `http://www.microsoft.com/sqlserver`.

If you do not think you need the extra features in a higher edition, go with what you need, then upgrade when you have the requirement. Visit the licensing model at `http://www.microsoft.com/sqlserver/en/us/get-sql-server/licensing.aspx` for the latest information.

Obtaining SQL Server 2012

Next we will look at how you acquire a copy of SQL Server, as it is not quite as straightforward you might expect. We hope you will evaluate it before you purchase, so first we will look at how to download the Evaluation Edition.

Evaluation

We always recommend that you try before you buy. Head to Microsoft's SQL Server 2012 web page at `http://www.microsoft.com/sqlserver` and you will find links to download the latest release. You require a Microsoft Live account to obtain your copy, but this is simply a matter of registering with an e-mail address. Once you have done this, you can download an ISO image for either the 32- or 64-bit system.

Retail

Depending on where in the world you live, it may be that Microsoft do not sell their software directly to you as a business. If you have an MSDN subscription then you will receive copies as soon as they are released. However, if you are lucky enough to be in charge of purchasing, then you could just buy your licenses from Amazon. We recommend that you search the web to find the best prices.

Navigating the Installation Process

Over the years, Microsoft has altered the installation process as more features have been added to the database engine and it can be a confusing path to navigate. However, do not be disheartened if you are unsure; over time we have met many sysadmins who have been uncertain how to install and configure SQL Server correctly. Even as an experienced DBA, installing is something you may not do that frequently.

> You are ready to install SQL Server 2012 with its new and exciting features. But wait a minute... before you upgrade your production environment, install it in development or test as a secondary instance and make sure any SQL Server feature changes are addressed before going live.

If you install SQL Server correctly from the beginning, this will help your long-term performance so we will focus on those areas that matter the most, in order to increase your performance.

If your SQL Server installation comes in ISO file format, you can install directly from it by using software to create a virtual CD/DVD drive which mounts the ISO file for you. This saves you burning a DVD. We like to use MagicDisk, as this is free and reliable. To download your free copy, point your browser at: `http://www.magiciso.com/tutorials/miso-magicdisc-overview.htm?=mdisc_hlp106`.

The setup wizard will alert you if there are additional requirements. You may need to install Windows Server 2008 SP2 or Windows Server 2008 R2 SP1 before installing SQL Server. If you are installing on your local Windows 7 machine, you will also need SP1. This takes about an hour to install.

Decide on the name of your Windows Server before you install SQL Server. If you want to change it, do this now before installing the database engine components. Changing the Windows name after installing SQL Server usually results in needless work and serious stress: linked servers, replication and mirroring may be affected and are more likely to break, as they will search for the original name of the server.

Once your Windows server is prepared, double-click on the `setup.exe` file to begin installing SQL Server. On the **Planning** screen, you will see links to help documentation, including release notes and how to upgrade from a previous version. Read and review as necessary, then click on the **Installation** link. Choose the option which best suits the installation you want. For a new installation, click on the top link: **New SQL Server stand-alone installation...**This will start the setup process:

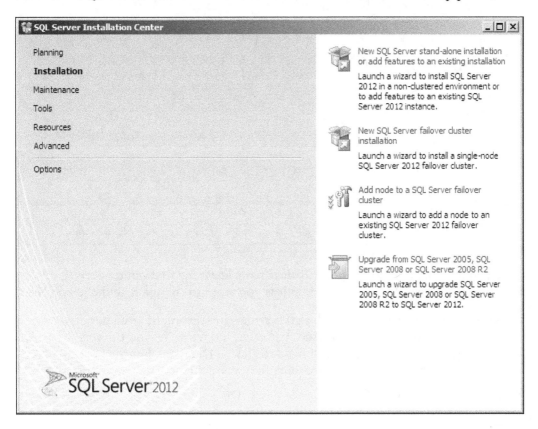

Enter your license key number or choose to run it as an evaluation (or install the Express Edition). On the next screen click to accept the software license terms. When you arrive at the **Setup Support Rules** screen, you will need to address any reported issues before proceeding.

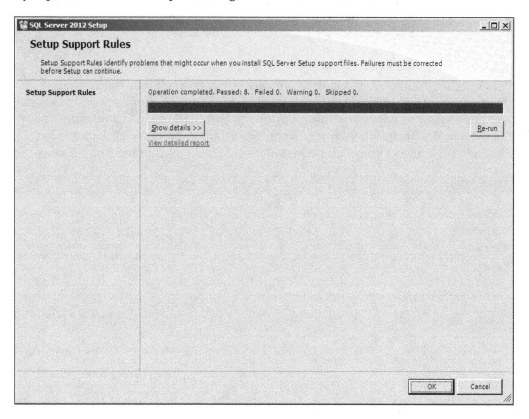

Once you are on the **Setup Support Role** screen, leave the first option of **SQL Server Feature Installation** checked, unless you want to change it, and click on **Next**.

The **Feature Selection** screen is where it becomes interesting. If you later discover there is a component you have missed, you need not worry as you can install it later on. Right now, you will at least need to choose **Database Engine Services**. Depending on which edition you are installing, you will have different options.

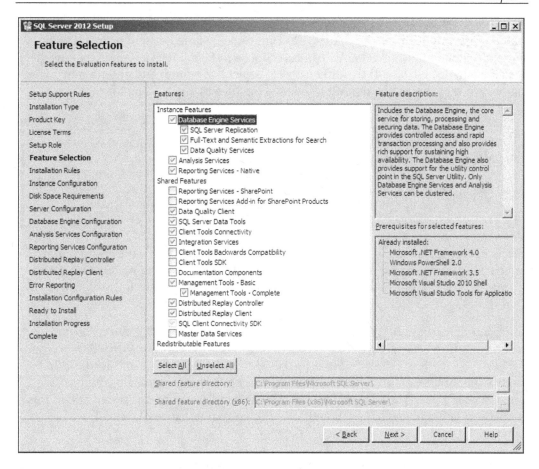

We are using Enterprise Edition and want to install **Analysis Services** (SSAS),
Reporting Services (SSRS), **Integration Services** (SSIS), **Data Quality Services**
(DQS), and **Master Data Services** (MDS), so that we can explore them later on
in this book. You could equally choose Developer Edition to install these features.

Business Intelligence Developer Studio (BIDS) has been replaced with **SQL Server
Data Tools**, which is used to develop reports, create packages, and build Analysis
Services objects such as cubes and dimensions. You will probably not want to install
this on your production system but in our case we have included it, again for the
purpose of this book.

In order to manage SQL Server, check the **Management Tools** option (SSMS).
Make your selections and click on **Next**.

Instance Configuration gives you two options: installing a default instance or a named instance. If this is the first SQL Server to be installed, it will be installed as a default instance automatically. You can choose to install it as a named instance if you wish; just click on the radio button to select this option and enter a new name. We will choose the default and leave the files in our C: directory.

> Install SQL Server on the same drive as your Operating System (OS), usually the C: drive, and put your data and logs files each on their own drive. As an absolute minimum, mirror all your drives using RAID 1, including the OS and SQL Server executables drive. If you want to increase your performance further, give tempdb its own drive. Tempdb is used not just for user queries, but also by SQL Server's internal operations. SSDs can speed up tempdb operations significantly.

Click on **Next** and wait while the setup calculates whether you have enough disk space. This may take a minute. We are now good to go, so click on **Next** and ring up the **Server Configuration** screen. We are now talking about Windows Active Directory (AD) accounts, passwords, and security.

For many DBAs, the biggest stumbling point when installing SQL Server is not knowing which service accounts to use. If you wish, you can use a different account for each service you install, but it is a good idea to set up at least one account that is dedicated to SQL Server. By using a separate account for each service, you isolate any issues if a password or service is compromised. However, the downside to this is that server engineers have a potentially higher maintenance overhead.

> Use a different account for your development and test servers to the one you use in production. This means you have no requirement to give the login to your developers, thereby restricting access to production systems.

The account that you use for SQL Server should have a strong password and preferably be limited to much less than local administrator rights (see the following tip). It is always a good idea to talk to your system administrator before proceeding, to make sure the account you use is set up correctly.

> This is an important point to note... Never use an account which is a domain admin account; always use a domain user account. Give only the security rights that are needed. There is a lot of information on TechNet, including the article Setting Up Windows Service Accounts, which is written specifically for SQL Server: http://technet.microsoft.com/en-us/library/ms143504.aspx.

Click on the **Account Name** to bring up the **Browse** option. Click again to bring up a window to allow you to choose another account:

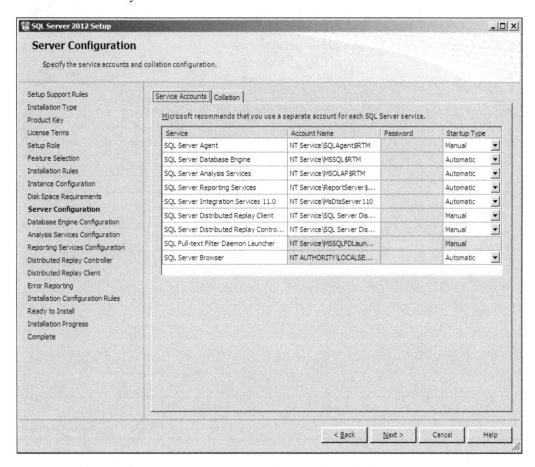

At this point, you may also want to change the startup options for SQL Server Agent and SQL Server Browser. If you intend to run any scheduled jobs, start SQL Agent. If you want to allow remote connections to your new database engine, SQL Browser may need to be running if you have any named instances installed. You can start or stop each service later on from the command line, using Services Management Console, SQL Server Configuration Manager, or from the Cluster Administrator tool if you are running SQL Server in a failover clustered environment.

Set up your accounts and move on to the **Database Engine Configuration** screen:

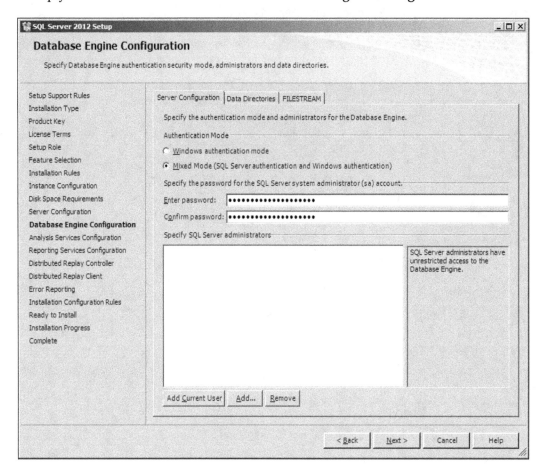

At this stage, choose Windows authentication if you only connect using AD authentication. If you have third-party applications using a username and password then you need to select **Mixed Mode**, and enter a password for the system administrator (sa) account. Add yourself and any other DBAs on your team who must have sysadmin access.

Click on Next. We are installing Analysis Services, so the screen for SSAS options appears. Choose your server mode, either **Multidimensional and Data Mining Mode** (your analytical objects are stored in the OLAP engine and queried using MDX) or **Tabular Mode** (your analytical objects are stored in the xVelocity engine and queried using DAX). If you are unsure, choose the default and if you need to run both modes, you can later install a separate instance to run in the other mode.

See *Chapter 4, Analysis Services,* to discover which Analysis Services model is already installed and running on your server.

Whichever mix of services you have chosen to install, you will eventually land on the **Error Reporting** screen. If you would like to help Microsoft improve SQL Server, leave the option checked to send error reports.

After we have passed the test for **Installation Configuration Rules**, we can now click on **Next** and move on to review what we are about to install. Once we are all set, we can finally click on the **Install** button. This takes a while so it is a good time to grab a coffee.

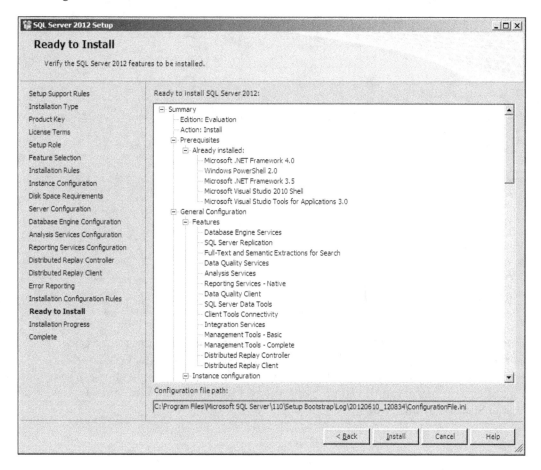

Based on the selection of the services and features, our installation took about an hour to complete on a desktop PC, but this will probably be a bit quicker on your servers! Be aware that once the setup has completed, you will be prompted to restart the server.

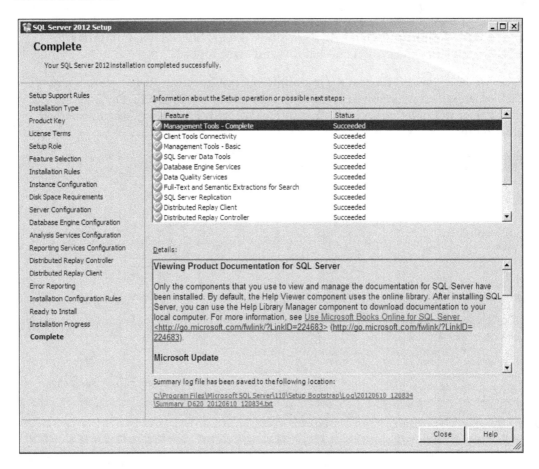

Once you have restarted your server, go to **Program Files** and open up **SQL Server 2012 Management Studio**. If, like us, you have been using SSMS for a while, you will be familiar with its look and feel. It may be a slight shock to see that Microsoft has given the UI an overhaul and it is now very similar to the Visual Studio 2010 interface:

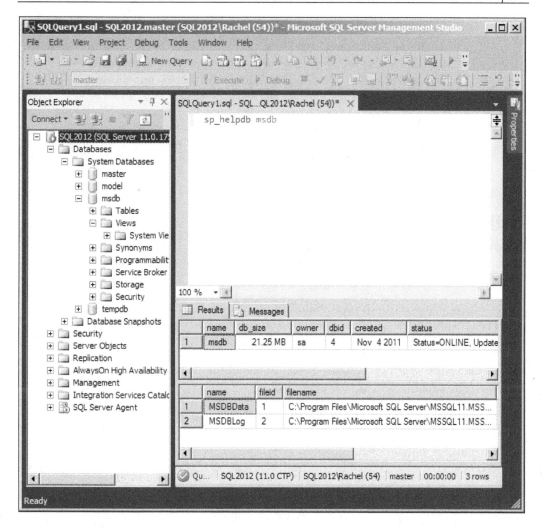

Note that Books Online (BOL) is no longer included with the installation media. You can download and install it separately or simply view it directly on the Microsoft website at `http://msdn.microsoft.com/en-us/library/ms130214.aspx`.

Now that you have successfully installed SQL Server, you need to know how to get the best out of it. We will be covering new features such as High Availability, columnstore indexes, and Distributed Replay later on in this book but right now it is important to think about security updates, patches, and service packs.

Using Twitter to Learn More

 A great way to keep up with security releases and find out about how your SQL Server works is to follow a few key Twitter profiles. Microsoft's Customer Support Service Engineers for SQL Server is a wonderful source of both news and information. You can read their blog at `http://blogs.msdn.com/b/psssql` and follow them on Twitter `@MicrosoftSQLCSS`. You can benefit from following Microsoft's main SQL Server Twitter account `@SQLServer`, as well as `@TechNet`.

Summary

In this chapter, we looked at the different editions of SQL Server available to us, from the Evaluation and Developer Editions, right up to the big iron Enterprise Edition.

We saw how you can download Evaluation Edition from the Microsoft website, and have the option to use the Developer Edition unless you are deploying to a production system, saving added expenditure on licensing costs.

In the next chapter, things become even more exciting as we look at the new administration features in SQL Server 2012.

2

SQL Server Administration

SQL Server's management tools have always been strong. Some would say they are the best in the relational database market. We would agree, but we would add that they are the best by a long way. This is good news for us because as DBAs and developers, we spend a lot of time using them. The more we get done and the better we do it, the happier our bosses will be.

While SQL Server's early tools were comparatively basic and un-integrated, the latest administration tools are exceptionally powerful; indeed there is little separation now between development and administration tools, arguably the way it should be.

In addition to this, the features that the tools can now administer have been vastly extended in SQL Server 2012. New security, contained databases, clustering, columnstore indexes, Distributed Replay and AlwaysOn High Availability features are new features in SQL Server 2012. Let's take a look.

Management Studio keyboard shortcuts

Differences in keyboard shortcuts between Microsoft products might be one of your major complaints. That feeling of "nothing works like it should" can be cause for discontent. SQL Server Management Studio has updated its appearance to match the Visual Studio 2010 IDE look and feel, and it is possible to utilize the keyboard shortcuts from Visual Studio 2010. From **Management Studio**, simply click on the **Tools** menu and select **Options**. An **Options** dialog box will open as shown in the following screenshot:

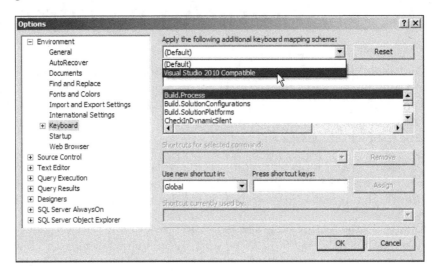

Make your shortcuts work for you to boost your personal productivity. Check out the following link for the full list of keyboard shortcuts in SQL Server 2012: http://msdn.microsoft.com/en-us/library/ms174205%28v=sql.110%29.aspx.

New Dynamic Management Views (DMVs)

At last! After years of pressure, Microsoft has finally responded to the DBA and developer community by including some very useful DMVs. These are accessible directly from T-SQL and can access hard-to-retrieve system information without having to revert to external **Windows Management Instrumentation (WMI)** calls and extended stored procedures.

Some of these DMVs were added as part of SQL Server 2008 R2, but we have included them here as they were not widely publicized and many sites will be migrating from SQL Server 2008 to SQL Server 2012 without hitting R2 on the way.

First though, there is a neat amendment to the `dm_exec_query_stats` DMV, which now has four shiny new columns detailing total, last number, maximum, and minimum rows returned by a query. These are very handy additions for troubleshooting bothersome queries. Run the following simple query to see cumulative statistics for cached query plans:

```
SELECT * FROM sys.dm_exec_query_stats
```

Downloading the example code

You can download the example code files for all Packt books you have purchased from your account at `http://www.packtpub.com`. If you purchased this book elsewhere, you can visit `http://www.packtpub.com/support` and register to have the files e-mailed directly to you.

Perhaps the least useful (until you really need it) DMV introduced with SQL Server 2012 is `sys.dm_server_memory_dumps`. This returns a simple list of any memory dumps that SQL Server has created, detailing filename, creation time, and size (in bytes) of the file. It is useful in troubleshooting scenarios on those (exceptionally rare) occasions when SQL Server creates a memory dump.

Another of the new DMVs introduced with SQL Server 2012 is as follows:

```
SELECT * FROM sys.dm_server_services
```

This query fetches information about the current SQL Server instance's Windows services, including information about whether the services are clustered, as shown in the following screenshot:

servicename	startup_type	startup_type_desc	status	status_desc	process_id	last_startup_time
SQL Server (MSSQLSERVER)	2	Automatic	4	Running	1952	2012-04-29 17:59:24
SQL Server Agent (MSSQLSERVER)	2	Automatic	4	Running	2676	NULL
SQL Full-text Filter Daemon Launch...	3	Manual	4	Running	2468	NULL

Hot on its tail is another useful DMV that grabs the SQL Server related information from the registry for all instances; not of everyday use, but certainly useful to anyone who has ever attempted to write a monitoring tool or perform custom auditing of their SQL Server environment:

```
SELECT * FROM sys.dm_server_registry
```

As shown in the following screenshot, this returns the registry keys and their name value pairs:

registry_key	value_name	value_data
HKLM\SYSTEM\CurrentControlSet\Services\MSSQLSERVER	ObjectName	NT Service\MSSQLSERVER
HKLM\SYSTEM\CurrentControlSet\Services\MSSQLSERVER	ImagePath	"C:\Program Files\Microsoft SQL Server\MSSQL11.M...
HKLM\SYSTEM\CurrentControlSet\Services\MSSQLSERVER	Start	2
HKLM\SYSTEM\CurrentControlSet\Services\SQLSERVERA...	ObjectName	NT Service\SQLSERVERAGENT
HKLM\SYSTEM\CurrentControlSet\Services\SQLSERVERA...	ImagePath	"C:\Program Files\Microsoft SQL Server\MSSQL11.M...
HKLM\SYSTEM\CurrentControlSet\Services\SQLSERVERA...	Start	2
HKLM\SYSTEM\CurrentControlSet\Services\SQLSERVERA...	DependOnService	MSSQLSERVER
HKLM\Software\Microsoft\Microsoft SQL Server\MSSQL11....	CurrentVersion	11.0.2100.60
HKLM\Software\Microsoft\Microsoft SQL Server\MSSQL11....	SQLArg0	-dC:\Program Files\Microsoft SQL Server\MSSQL11.M...
HKLM\Software\Microsoft\Microsoft SQL Server\MSSQL11....	SQLArg1	-eC:\Program Files\Microsoft SQL Server\MSSQL11.M...
HKLM\Software\Microsoft\Microsoft SQL Server\MSSQL11....	SQLArg2	-lC:\Program Files\Microsoft SQL Server\MSSQL11.M...
HKLM\Software\Microsoft\Microsoft SQL Server\MSSQL11....	TcpDynamicPorts	1434
HKLM\Software\Microsoft\Microsoft SQL Server\MSSQL11....	DisplayName	TCP/IP

 You can run these queries just as you would run any other and can execute them against multiple servers, then UNION them together to compare results. To discover some useful operating system level information, execute the following query:

```
SELECT * FROM sys.dm_os_windows_info
```

As shown in the following screenshot, this simple query provides us with helpful details of the operating system that can be used for auditing your servers:

windows_release	windows_service_pack_level	windows_sku	os_language_version
6.1	Service Pack 1	1	1033

The new OS Volume Stats DMV

Finally there is a DMV which was quietly introduced in SQL Server 2008 R2, but is worthy of another mention here, as it returns information about the file system for any given file for any database.

This is particularly useful to the DBA who runs their SQL Server on a **Storage Area Network (SAN)**, which is becoming more commonplace. The following example returns data about the log file (`file_id`: **2**) for the master database (`database_id`: **1**):

```
SELECT * FROM sys.dm_os_volume_stats (1,2)
```

Run this query and you will see something similar to the following screenshot, which details the file type, size and how much space is remaining:

database_id	file_id	volume...	volume_id	logi...	file_system_type	total_bytes	available_bytes	supports_compression
1	2	C:\	\\?\Volum...		NTFS	319965622272	11963912192	1

Spatial indexes

Along with a large number of enhancements to T-SQL's support for spatial data types, Microsoft has quietly added in a few administrative improvements too. Chief amongst these is the build time for spatial indexes on point data, which is four to five times faster than in SQL Server 2008; this is significant if you are administering tables with millions of rows of point data. The STDistance and STBuffer functions have also been better optimized for performance.

Additionally you can now compress spatial indexes with either row or page compression. The syntax is the same as non-spatial data indexes:

```
CREATE SPATIAL INDEX idxPostalCodePoints
ON PostalCodePoints (Latitude) USING GEOGRAPHY_GRID
WITH (DATA_COMPRESSION = PAGE)
```

Or use:

```
WITH (DATA_COMPRESSION = ROW)
```

Two new stored procedures have been introduced to evaluate spatial data distribution in a column:

```
sp_help_spatial_geography_histogram    PostalCodePoints, Latitude,
1000, 100
sp_help_spatial_geometry_histogram    PostalCodePoints, Latitude, 1000,
100
```

The parameters in the above examples are table name, column name, cell size and sample size.

 A great article on all of the new spatial data features and improvements in SQL Server 2012 can be found at: http://social. technet.microsoft.com/wiki/contents/articles/4136. aspx#Compression_for_Spatial_Indexes.

Columnstore indexes

In SQL Server 2012, data is still stored with each row stored after the previous row on each page in the database. From a data storage perspective, nothing has changed. However, what columnstore technology has introduced to SQL Server 2012 is the columnstore index. This is an index created just like any other, but it stores index data in a highly compressed, column-wise fashion. For certain classes of queries, particularly those found in Kimball-design star schemas, columnstore indexes make a lot of sense. Typical performance gains of between 10x - 100x performance can be possible for certain queries, so they are worth investigating, as they may provide an alternative to a very costly hardware upgrade.

Note that no special hardware is needed to use columnstore indexes, they are a part of the database engine and can be created on any standard server.

Creating a columnstore index

Creating a columnstore index on an existing table is very simple. For example, for a table with the following definition:

```
CREATE TABLE Customer
(
    CustomerName varchar(200) NULL,
    DateOfBirth datetime NULL,
    Sex char(10) NULL,
    Salary int NULL,
    LoanAmount int NULL
)
```

Although you can specify only those columns you want to include, you would usually create a columnstore index across all of the columns using the following query:

```
CREATE NONCLUSTERED COLUMNSTORE INDEX csidxCustomer
ON Customer (CustomerName, DateOfBirth, Sex, Salary, LoanAmount)
```

To drop a columnstore index, use the same syntax as you would normally use:

```
DROP INDEX Customer.csidxCustomer
```

Likewise, disabling a columnstore index can be done in the same way:

```
ALTER INDEX csidxCustomer ON Customer DISABLE
```

This can easily be reversed by rebuilding the index, which assumes the same columns as when the index was initially built:

```
ALTER INDEX csidxCustomer ON Customer REBUILD
```

However, note that as the columnstore index is built in memory, it is possible that under low memory conditions the following error might be seen:

```
Low memory condition:
The statement has been terminated.
Msg 8645, Level 17, State 1, Line 1
A timeout occurred while waiting for memory resources to execute the
query in resource pool 'default' (2).
Rerun the query.
```

If this error is seen frequently, is may be worth assessing if your SQL Server has sufficient memory allocated to it.

Restrictions

However, columnstore indexes do have some restrictions. The most limiting restriction at present is that they cannot be updated, and as such any updates applied to a table will fail. If you do try to perform an insert, update or delete, you will see the following error message, even if the query affects zero rows:

```
INSERT statement failed because data cannot be updated in a table with
a columnstore index.
```

However, the remainder of the error message comes to our rescue:

```
Consider disabling the columnstore index before issuing the INSERT
statement, then re-building the columnstore index after INSERT is
complete.
```

This of course is not an acceptable thing to do in OLTP databases. However, in a copy of a database used for reporting, or for a data warehouse, where the database may only be restored, or built once per business day, it may be acceptable to drop and re-create the index. Indeed, in many data warehouse implementations, it is common practice to drop all indexes, populate a table using ETL, and then re-create the indexes after the load. This not only improves the load time (as the indexes do not have to be maintained), but also improves query performance whilst the data warehouse is being used for complex reports, as the index more accurately reflects the data it was originally built for.

Your corporate budget will also determine whether you can utilize columnstore technology. Specifically, only the Enterprise Edition and Developer Edition currently offer columnstore support. Like many other features, we expect this to filter down to the Standard and Business Intelligence editions at some point in the future. We were surprised that they were not included in the Business Intelligence edition, as they are perfectly suited to star schema performance acceleration.

Columns of certain data types cannot be included as part of a columnstore index. However, the columnstore index can still be built on the table for the remaining rows that are not of these specific types:

```
binary and varbinary
datetimeoffset with precision > 2
decimal or numeric with precision > 18
hierarchyid
image
sqlvariant
text and ntext
timestamp
uniqueidentifier
varchar(max) and nvarchar(max)
xml
```

That is quite a list. However, for data warehouses that utilize star schema designs, this is rarely going to cause a problem, as the columns that contain these data types can easily be omitted from the create index query.

Other restrictions include the inability to create a columnstore index on computed and sparse columns, or on an indexed view. Columnstore indexes cannot be filtered, and only one can be created on each table.

You might also be asking, "Can I have a clustered columnstore index?". The answer is "No". If you think about it, it soon becomes obvious why this is the case. A clustered index contains the actual pages that data is stored on. In order for a clustered index to be a columnstore index, each of those pages would have to hold data in a column-wise, rather than row-wise fashion. Whilst this is possible, and there are databases that offer this technology, to do so in SQL Server, which stores data pages in a row-wise order would require a rather drastic change to the core database engine and the way that it stores and accesses data.

However, for certain analytical and data warehouse applications, data stored in a columnstore fashion would provide certain performance advantages. It is an intriguing possibility that, perhaps in a future release, Microsoft might provide the capability to create tables, or even entire databases which by default store data in a column-wise fashion for performance benefits, and which can automatically detect and switch between those that use column based storage and those that use the more usual row based storage.

Looking to the future, we are certain that columnstore indexes will evolve into a more and more useful component in the SQL Server performance toolkit. Specifically, we would expect to see updateable columnstore indexes at some point in the future, which will open up interesting competition in the OLTP world.

 We have only described the tip of what can be learned about columnstore indexes here. We highly recommend Microsoft's own SQL Server Columnstore FAQ on the TechNet site at `http://social.technet.microsoft.com/wiki/contents/articles/3540.sql-server-columnstore-index-faq-en-us.aspx`.

This has an impressive wealth of content, plus links to dozens of sites, white papers, performance tests and videos, and we would highly recommend that you pay it a visit.

Contained databases

Contained databases are a new concept in SQL Server 2012. Currently, if a database is moved from one server to another, or even one instance of SQL Server to another, in most cases the applications that are associated with it cannot use it immediately, even if that database is a secondary database or mirror for the principal.

Logins, scheduled jobs and endpoints all have to be created, and are sometimes not identified until a problem occurs. This can occupy a large amount of time for the DBA or developer, both in troubleshooting the problem and fixing it.

However, SQL Server 2012 doesn't have contained databases. What it does have, at least in the initial RTM version, is partially contained databases. This release contains the initial stepping stone to the holy grail of fully contained databases, where all the metadata associated with a database is stored (or "contained") within the database itself, rather than at the system database level, for instance in the master or msdb databases.

While partially contained databases will make our jobs easier, they will certainly not solve every administrative headache, at least not yet.

Fortunately, Microsoft has provided a DMV that lists any objects that do not comply with containment rules for the current database. With a little tweaking to return the name of the object that isn't contained, we can obtain some useful information:

```
SELECT object_name (major_id), *
FROM sys.dm_db_uncontained_entities
```

Items that are not contained will be objects such as tables, but principals such as logins, assemblies, data types, indexes, and triggers are among others that are also reported. For a full list of features that cannot be considered as part of a contained database, see the MSDN web page at http://msdn.microsoft.com/en-us/library/ff929118%28v=sql.110%29.aspx.

Making an existing database partially contained

To make an existing database partially contained is a quick, three-step process:

1. Make a SQL Server instance level change to allow a contained database to authenticate with the database engine. This is done as follows:

   ```
   sp_configure 'contained database authentication', 1
   reconfigure
   ```

2. If you intend to use the GUI tools to change the containment type, you will need to kill all connections to the database that you want to make partially contained. Note that this is only necessary when taking a database from non-contained to partially contained; setting it back to non-contained does not require this step, nor does it apply if you use T-SQL to change the containment mode to partial.

3. Finally, set the database to partially contained mode. This can be done using the T-SQL command:

   ```
   ALTER DATABASE test
   SET containment = PARTIAL
   ```

   Or to revert it, use the following:

   ```
   SET containment = NONE
   ```

Or it can be performed through the GUI tools, as shown in the following screenshot:

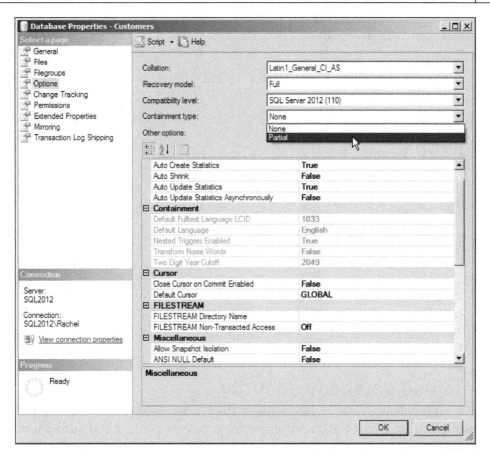

Migrating your logins to a contained database

Once your existing database has been converted to a contained database, you are
left with the task of migrating your logins. These logins can be easily migrated to
a partially contained database level using the following T-SQL code:

```
DECLARE @UserName sysname
DECLARE csrUsers cursor
FOR
SELECT      dbprin.name
FROM sys.database_principals AS dbprin
    INNER JOIN
    sys.server_principals AS svrprin
ON  dbprin.sid = svrprin.sid
```

```
WHERE dbprin.authentication_type = 1
AND svrprin.is_disabled = 0

OPEN csrUsers
FETCH NEXT
FROM csrUsers
INTO @UserName

WHILE @@fetch_status = 0
  BEGIN
        exec sp_migrate_user_to_contained
        @username = @UserName,
        @rename = N'keep_name',
        @disablelogin = N'disable_login'
          -- disable the server level login
    FETCH NEXT
     FROM csrUsers
     INTO @UserName
  END
CLOSE csrUsers
DEALLOCATE csrUsers
```

Contained database security

There are a number of security issues that a DBA must observe when utilizing contained databases. For instance, because users have to connect and authenticate at the database level, if a weak password policy was in place on the server where the contained database was created, and that database is subsequently moved to a server with a stricter security policy, the database will still have the weaker password in place from the instance where it was created. This circumvents the password policy of the more secure server.

> A good place to start reading about threats to a partially contained database is on the MSDN site at: http://msdn.microsoft.com/en-us/library/ff929055%28v=sql.110%29.aspx.

In addition to this, because the password hashes for the SQL Server users that are allowed to connect to the database are now contained inside the database rather than in the **master** database, anyone who has access to the database can perform a dictionary attack. They no longer need access to the server where the login previously resided, just a copy of the database files, or a backup of the database.

This obviously puts emphasis on the DBA and the system administrators to observe stronger file system security procedures or, at the very least, only create users within the contained database that rely upon Windows security to authenticate rather than SQL Server security.

Security management

There are a number of new enhancements to security in SQL Server 2012. Keeping your data secure is always high priority, so in the following section we will explore how these features can help you and how to put them in place.

Default schemas for groups

You can now define a default schema for a group, which most DBAs use to simplify administration. This avoids implicit schema creation, so when a user creates an object, it is created under the group schema instead of under **database owner (dbo)**. This eases administration and saves objects from being created in the wrong schema. Furthermore, it avoids the possibility of a query using the wrong schema and returning incorrect results. This was one of the most requested security features for SQL Server 2012, so well done Microsoft for responding!

User defined server roles

Roles can already be created at the database level, but now SQL Server allows roles to be created at the server level too. This allows a finer level of control where, for instance, temporary DBA staff can be granted most server-level sysadmin privileges, but denied the ability to alter logins or alter audit permissions.

All this can be done through the CREATE/ALTER/DROP SERVER ROLE commands, or through the GUI with a right-click on the **Server Roles** node, where a new menu item has appeared, as shown in the following screenshot:

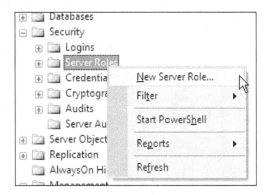

This brings up a new dialog box, as shown in the following screenshot:

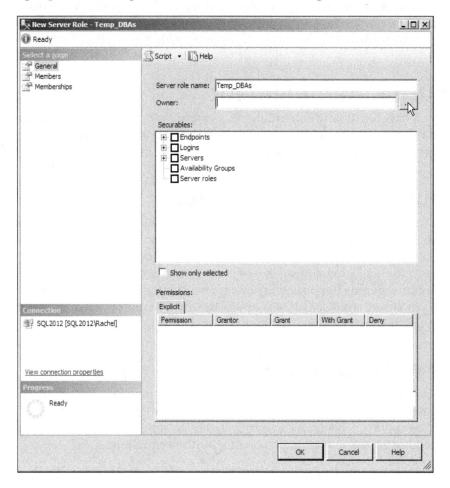

Alternatively, server roles can be administered through simple T-SQL commands. An example follows, which creates a server role called TEMPDBAROLE for a DBA with the login name ContractDBA, who might be covering while the full-time DBA is on vacation.

The same could be applied to a junior or probationary production DBA. The TEMPDBAROLE is then permitted view server state permissions, as well as view permissions on any database and any object's definition. However, it is denied access to altering trace information.

Finally, the temporary DBA's login is added to the new server role to give them the restricted set of sysadmin permissions, something which was previously very difficult to achieve, using the following code:

```
USE master
GO
CREATE SERVER ROLE TEMPDBAROLE AUTHORIZATION sa
GRANT VIEW SERVER STATE TO TEMPDBAROLE
GRANT VIEW ANY DATABASE TO TEMPDBAROLE
GRANT VIEW ANY DEFINITION TO TEMPDBAROLE
DENY ALTER TRACE TO TEMPDBAROLE

ALTER SERVER ROLE  TEMPDBAROLE ADD MEMBER ContractDBA
```

SQL Server Audit enhancements

SQL Audit can now be used on all versions of SQL Server, albeit with a few limitations. It is also more resilient, with the ability to recover from network failures and to automatically restart after a server shutdown. Microsoft has provided an audit event stored procedure with the following parameters:

```
EXEC sp_audit_write @user_defined_event_id, @succeeded,
@user_defined_info
```

For instance, sp_audit_write will write a user defined event into the audit log, which can be viewed through the SQL Server Management Studio log file viewer:

```
EXEC sp_audit_write 12345, 1, 'Audit Event Text'
```

> A great forum on SQL Server security is hosted by Microsoft at: http://social.msdn.microsoft.com/Forums/en-gb/sqlsecurity/threads.

Master Data Services (MDS)

Microsoft has added plenty of new features to Master Data Services in this 2012 release. If you are already using the service, then you will know that it is possible to write an entire book devoted purely to MDS. To end this chapter, we will quickly review some of the new features in MDS.

It is now easier to install MDS, as you do this during the database engine installation process and no longer need a separate installer. As with other additional services, such as Integration Services and Reporting Services, you don't need to install this the first time you install the database engine. Just run through the installation setup again and choose to add new features.

To use the Master Data Manager web application, you need to install Silverlight 5.0 on the client machine. Not surprisingly, Silverlight is not part of the SQL Server installation, but you can easily download it from the Microsoft site. Microsoft has also improved the Master Data Manager web user interface (UI), which can now be cropped for a better presentation display inside web sites, including SharePoint.

If your users access data through SharePoint, there is a new MDS Add-in for Excel that will be advantageous. The Add-in allows you to create a shortcut query file to connect and load frequently-used data from the MDS repository into the Add-in. The query file is built using XML, which means it can be saved to SharePoint for the benefit of other users.

The Excel Add-in allows you to manage your master data. You can load a filtered data-set from your MDS database, work with it inside Excel, and then publish it back to the database. Administrators can use the Add-in to create new entities and attributes. In order to load data, you now have to open a new worksheet.

Improvements have been made to increase your visible workspace so that when you load data, the Master Data Explorer pane automatically closes. Furthermore, information about the currently active worksheet is displayed in a single row at the top of the sheet.

Shortcut query files hold information regarding the server, model and version, entity, and any filters that were applied. The Excel Add-in for MDS 2012 includes a new toolbar button and with just a couple of clicks, you can email the shortcut query file to another user via Microsoft Outlook.

A great new feature in this Add-in is the ability to check that you are not adding duplicate records prior to adding more data to MDS. It takes advantage of **SQL Server Data Quality Services (DQS)** to compare the data in MDS with the data from the incoming source. DQS provides suggestions for updating your data and a percent of confidence that changes are correct. In the previous version of MDS, you were required to load members and attributes into MDS in separate batches. You can now load all the members and attributes for an entity in a single operation.

Summary

In this chapter we began with a quick look at SQL Server Management Studio, followed by the new DMVs. Then we explored SQL Server's new security features and discovered contained databases—which we will no doubt see more improvements being applied to in future editions.

In the next chapter we will explore the new T-SQL functions, examine error handling improvements and look at the new string, datetime and analytical functions.

3
Transact SQL

IBM created SQL in the 1970s as a language to query the relational database they had invented. Later, Oracle came to the market with PL/SQL in the 1980s, followed swiftly by T-SQL, which has been with us right since the Sybase SQL server days and now encompasses the SQL-92 ANSI standard. Thankfully Microsoft has again extended it for us in SQL Server 2012, adding new functionality as they see appropriate. While some think it is not acceptable to write non-standard SQL, remember that even simple DDL commands such as CREATE INDEX are an extension.

This means it is very easy to write non-standard SQL and that is no different to any of the other major database vendors. In fact, it contributes to driving future standards without which SQL would stagnate. But for us, it means a richer, easier to use language with features that would otherwise be difficult to implement, particularly from a performance perspective. Furthermore if we have no plans to port our applications to another database platform, there really is very little reason to take international standards into consideration.

In this chapter, we look at T-SQL's new string and datetime, formatting, and error-handling abilities. We are going to explore the new FileTable table type and try out the new analytical functions with some simple code samples to start you off. You will also be introduced to SQL Server Data Tools (SSDT), the replacement for BIDS. There is plenty to cover in this chapter, so shall we begin?

String functions

With SQL Server 2012 Microsoft has introduced two new string functions, bringing the total to 25. String functions perform an operation on a string value that you input, returning another string (or sometimes numeric) value. They are also referred to as **scalar functions**, which mean they operate on a single value and return just a single value.

New to 2012 are the CONCAT() and FORMAT() functions. Let us take a look at what they do and explore some real world examples of how you might use them in your day to day T-SQL programming.

CONCAT

As you might have already guessed, the job of CONCAT is to perform a concatenation operation. Pass CONCAT a number of string arguments and it will concatenate, or join them together and return an output string.

The basic structure is as follows:

```
CONCAT ( string_value_1,  string_value_1 [, string_value_n ] )
```

Now if you are thinking, "Is this really of any use? Surely I can do that already using the concatenation operator?", then hold tight; there is a really useful feature to this function which we will explore in just a minute. Let us now create a temporary table and add a couple of records:

```
CREATE TABLE #Customer
(
    FirstName varchar(30) NOT NULL,
    MiddleName varchar(30) NULL,
    LastName varchar(30) NOT NULL
)


INSERT INTO #Customer
VALUES ('Rachel', 'Jane', 'Clements'), ('Jon', NULL, 'Reade')
```

We have our customer table, so now let us use the CONCAT function to return the full name of our customers:

```
SELECT CONCAT(FirstName + ' ', MiddleName + ' ', LastName) AS
CustomerName
FROM #Customer
```

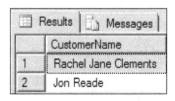

This returns the full names of our two customers, just as you would expect. Now, this is where the function really shows its worth. If we run the following statement:

```
SELECT FirstName + ' ' + MiddleName + ' ' + LastName AS CustomerName
FROM #Customer
```

You are probably expecting the results to be the same as the preceding one. If you are, you would be wrong. Take a look at the actual result as follows:

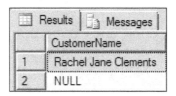

As you can see, our second customer, who doesn't have a middle name, is returned as a NULL value. Using the CONCAT function we can return a concatenation of values, allowing for NULL values. Another perfect and rather common use for this would be an address table that has the columns Address1 and Address2. Not every record will have a value for Address2.

FORMAT

The formatting of dates across different cultures has been a bug bear for developers since the dawn of programming. With an increasing need to consider multinational customers in this Internet age, designing systems to accommodate different cultures is vital and yet difficult to do right. A date format in one culture (en-US) of MM/DD/YYYY mixed with that of another (en-GB) that uses DD/MM/YYYY can cause havoc. In one country the date 10-08-2012 is in October, and in the other it is in August.

For locale-related formatting of strings and numbers, the new FORMAT function comes to the rescue. FORMAT will take any culture supported by the .NET Framework, though as you can see from the following statement, this is an optional argument:

```
FORMAT ( value, format [, culture ] )
```

The first parameter (*value*) is the variable to apply the formatting to. The second argument, format, is the format of the value. Take care with the format argument, as this must be a supported .NET Framework format. *Culture* is the locale you would like to apply to the value. If you choose not to supply a culture, the function will use that of the current session.

So let us look at the date 10/08/2012. We are in the UK, so this is 10th August, 2012. If you are in the US, or another country that uses MM/DD/YYYY you will be thinking, "Wait, this date is in October". We will use the FORMAT function to convert it:

```
-- UK date is 10 August 2012
DECLARE @MyDate datetime = '10/08/2012'
SELECT FORMAT(@MyDate, 'dd/mm/yyyy', 'en-US') AS NewDate
```

This is returned as follows:

FORMAT is not just for dates; it can be used for time, money, and decimal locale conversions too.

> If SQL Server doesn't have a built in function to do precisely what you need, don't forget you can create your own, customizing it just the way you want, using your own business rules.
>
> If you would like to discover more about SQL Server 2012 functions, point your browser at: http://msdn.microsoft.com/en-us/library/ms174318(v=sql.110).aspx.

Datetime functions

New functions that make datetime variables easier to handle are always welcome. With SQL Server 2012 there are a number of new functions that we think will really make your programming life much easier. We will explore a number of examples so you can quickly understand how to use them in your everyday code.

EOMONTH

Firstly we will start with the end of month function or, more specifically, EOMONTH, as you will soon learn. This function does exactly what it says, returning the last day of the month you specify. This will no doubt come as a pleasant addition to anyone who runs financial calculations. The syntax is as follows:

```
DECLARE @MyDate datetime
SET @MyDate = '05/17/2012'
SELECT EOMONTH (@MyDate) AS LastDayOfTheMonth
```

As you can see from the following result this returns the last day of the month of May:

We have written this book in a leap year which, as you know, generally only happens every four years, coinciding with the Olympics. This function removes the need to code around the extra day that the leap year brings. How great is that?

Now you are probably thinking, "That is pretty cool, but can it do anything else?" Actually it can. There is another parameter value you can feed in to return the end of the month, either in the past or future. Let us see what the end of month date is six months on from our test date, simply by adding in another parameter:

```
DECLARE @MyDatedatetime
SET @MyDate = '05/17/2012'
SELECT EOMONTH (@MyDate, 6) AS LastDayOfTheMonth
```

Six months on and the last day of the month is as follows:

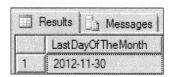

By utilizing a negative number, we can go back six months:

```
DECLARE @MyDate datetime
SET @MyDate = '05/17/2012'
SELECT EOMONTH (@MyDate, -6) AS LastDayOfTheMonth
```

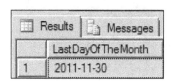

DATEFROMPARTS

Next up is the DATEFROMPARTS function which accepts year, month and day parameters and returns them as a date variable. Currently your code for returning these parameters as a date would probably look something like this:

```
DECLARE @Year int, @Month int, @Day int
SET @Year = 2012
SET @Month = 04
SET @Day = 09
SELECT CONVERT(datetime,CONVERT(varchar(10),@Year) + '/' +
CONVERT(varchar(10),@Month) + '/' +
CONVERT(varchar(10),@Day),103) AS MyDate
```

This would result in the following:

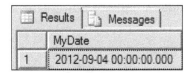

As you can see from the preceding code, there is a lot of work converting from integer values to varchar and back to a datetime value. What if there was a simpler way to do this? Well now there is. Compare the above syntax to the following T-SQL using the new DATEFROMPARTS function:

```
DECLARE @Year int, @Month int, @Day int
SET @Year = 2012
SET @Month = 09
SET @Day = 23
SELECT DATEFROMPARTS (@Year, @Month, @Day) AS MyDate
```

You pass in date "parts" and this function converts them to a date for you:

TIMEFROMPARTS

The TIMEFROMPARTS function works in exactly the same way, but instead of passing in the year, month and day, as you have probably guessed, you pass in time parameters instead:

```
DECLARE @Hour int, @Minutes int, @Seconds int,
@FractionsOfASecond int, @SecondsPrecision int
SET @Hour = 15
SET @Minutes = 23
SET @Seconds = 47
SET @FractionsOfASecond = 500
SET @SecondsPrecision = 3
SELECT TIMEFROMPARTS (@Hour, @Minutes, @Seconds,
@FractionsOfASecond, @SecondsPrecision) AS MyTime
```

The result is a time variable as shown in the following screenshot:

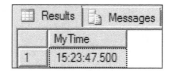

DATETIMEFROMPARTS

You can combine time and date with the DATETIMEFROMPARTS function and this will return a datetime variable to you. Again this works in the same way as the two previous functions:

```
DECLARE @Year int, @Month int, @Day int, @Hour int,
DECLARE @Minutes int, @Seconds int, @MilliSeconds int
SET @Year = 2012
SET @Month = 07
SET @Day = 23
SET @Hour = 17
SET @Minutes = 27
SET @Seconds = 49
SET @MilliSeconds = 0

SELECT DATETIMEFROMPARTS (@Year, @Month, @Day, @Hour, @Minutes,
@Seconds, @MilliSeconds) AS MyDateTime
```

The result is as follows:

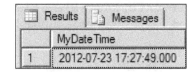

There are another couple of functions in this new group, DATETIME2FROMPARTS and SMALLDATETIMEFROMPARTS. These work in the same way, but as their names suggest, they return datetime2 and smalldatetime variables respectively.

DATETIMEOFFSETFROMPARTS

The final function we will look at allows you to add additional parameters to show the offset of hours and minutes so you can use datetimes across different time zones.

Take a look at the following code:

```
DECLARE @Year int, @Month int, @Day int
DECLARE @Hour int, @Minutes int, @Seconds int
DECLARE @FractionsOfASecond int
DECLARE @HourOffSet int, @MinuteOffSet int

SET @Year = 2012
SET @Month = 02
SET @Day = 26

SET @Hour = 15
SET @Minutes = 57
SET @Seconds = 49
SET @FractionsOfASecond = 500
SET @HourOffSet = 7
SET @MinuteOffSet = 30

SELECT DATETIMEOFFSETFROMPARTS (@Year, @Month, @Day, @Hour
@Minutes, @Seconds, @FractionsOfASecond, @HourOffSet,
@MinuteOffSet, 3) AS MyTimeZone
```

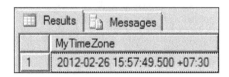

As you can see, added to the date and time we have fed into the function, the result appends the offset of the time zone. If you are dealing with businesses or customers on an international level, this function will be really helpful to you.

Conversion functions

SQL Server 2012 introduces some useful conversion functions that will help you avoid errors when dealing with different data types. We will use easy-to-understand examples so you can see how beneficial they are.

TRY_PARSE

TRY_PARSE doesn't look too useful on surface, but as we will soon see it has a very useful specialist niche.

The basic syntax of TRY_PARSE is as follows:

```
SELECT TRY_PARSE (string AS datatype)
```

Each of the following will return a NULL, as the value passed in the string does not convert to a value of the data type specified as the second parameter:

```
SELECT TRY_PARSE ('SQL Server 2012' AS datetime) AS MyDateTime
SELECT TRY_PARSE ('SQL Server 2012' AS decimal) AS MyDecimal
SELECT TRY_PARSE ('ABC' AS float) AS MyFloat
```

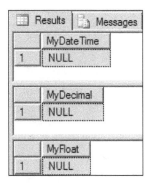

However, all of the following will return a date or numeric value equivalent to the string value:

```
SELECT TRY_PARSE ('03-07-2012' AS datetime) AS MyDateTime
SELECT TRY_PARSE ('2012' AS decimal) AS MyDecimal1
SELECT TRY_PARSE ('2012.0' AS decimal) AS MyDecimal2
SELECT TRY_PARSE ('2012.0' AS float) AS MyFloat
```

Note how the decimal and float checks return integer values rather than values of the requested data type:

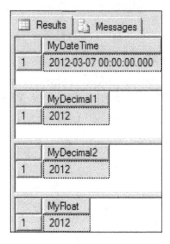

TRY_PARSE looks like a solution in search of a problem, but it is really handy for data cleansing and dirty data detection.

Consider the following simple example where data from a legacy system has to be loaded into a varchar or nvarchar column as, although it should only contain integer values, it actually has alphabetic characters in some of the rows:

```
CREATE TABLE DataToBeCleansed
(
   ID int IDENTITY (1,1),
   IntegerDataToBeCleansednvarchar(3)
)
GO

INSERT INTO DataToBeCleansed (IntegerDataToBeCleansed)
VALUES    ('1'),
    ('2'),
    ('E'),
    ('4'),
    ('5'),
    ('6'),
    ('L'),
    ('8'),
    ('9'),
    ('10')
GO
```

The table now contains the following values:

```
SELECT * FROM DataToBeCleansed
```

	ID	IntegerDataToBeCleansed
1	1	1
2	2	2
3	3	E
4	4	4
5	5	5
6	6	6
7	7	L
8	8	8
9	9	9
10	10	10

Now that we have loaded the data, we can easily split out the integer data from the non-integer data:

```
-- finds those values which are not true integers
SELECT     ID, IntegerDataToBeCleansed
INTO       RowsToBeCleansed
FROM       DataToBeCleansed
WHERE      TRY_PARSE(IntegerDataToBeCleansed AS int) IS NULL
GO
SELECT * FROM RowsToBeCleansed
```

This then yields the following rows into the RowsToBeCleansed table:

	ID	IntegerDataToBeCleansed
1	3	E
2	7	L

Furthermore we can uncover all of those rows that are valid:

```
SELECT  ID, IntegerDataToBeCleansed
INTO    CleansedData
FROM       DataToBeCleansed
WHERE      TRY_PARSE(IntegerDataToBeCleansed as int) IS NOT NULL
GO
SELECT * FROM CleansedData
```

	ID	IntegerDataToBeCleansed
1	1	1
2	2	2
3	4	4
4	5	5
5	6	6
6	8	8
7	9	9
8	10	10

Now how easy is that?

PARSE

It might seem odd to examine PARSE after TRY_PARSE. However, now that you have seen an example of TRY_PARSE in action, you can more easily understand how it works where PARSE would not. If we take one of the previous queries and modify it slightly:

```
SELECT ID, IntegerDataToBeCleansed
FROM       DataToBeCleansed
WHERE      PARSE(IntegerDataToBeCleansed AS int) IS NULL
```

You can now see that the query fails when it hits the rows where the string value cannot be parsed into an integer value, returning the following message:

```
Msg 9819, Level 16, State 1, Line 1
Error converting string value 'E' into data type int using culture ''.
```

In summary, use PARSE when you are sure of the quality of the data and use TRY_PARSE when you suspect or know that the data may contain values of an undesirable type.

Note that the error message reported *...using culture*. The culture setting for both `PARSE` and `TRY_PARSE` defaults to the language of the current session on which the query is being executed. This is most easily understood using the classic US/British datetime format:

```
SELECT   PARSE ('01/03/2012' AS DATETIME USING 'en-GB') AS GBDate
SELECT   PARSE ('01/03/2012' AS DATETIME USING 'en-US') AS USDate
```

 Are you working with international data? Take advantage of the new culture functionality and see a full list of supported culture settings at: `http://msdn.microsoft.com/en-us/library/hh213316%28v=sql.110%29.aspx`.

IIF

IIF is an inline conditional statement, just like most modern programming languages have had for years now. You pass an expression that can evaluate to either true or false to the function and it returns one value for true and another for false. As it is so easy to use, we will look at a very simple example here:

```
DECLARE @YourName nvarchar(20) = 'Jon'
DECLARE @MyName nvarchar(20) = 'Jon'
SELECT   IIF (@YourName = @MyName, 'Same person.',
'Different people.') AS NameMatch
```

If `@YourName` and `@MyName` match, then the result will be **Same person**. If they don't match, the result will be **Different people**:

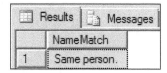

Now let us pass in two different values and see how this works:

```
DECLARE @YourName nvarchar(20) = 'Rachel'
DECLARE @MyName nvarchar(20) = 'Jon'
SELECT IIF (@YourName = @MyName, 'Same person.',
'Different people.') AS NameMatch
```

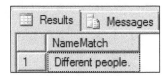

Take note though that you cannot use IIF as the first statement of a control-flow construct, it is designed *purely* for in-line decisions.

IIF is very useful where a straightforward comparison or transformation into one of two values has to be made on-the-fly. A great place to use this is in Reporting Services queries to tidy up the output for the end user without having to resort to the use of the more cumbersome and long winded CASE statement.

OFFSET and FETCH

OFFSET and FETCH are two new clauses introduced in SQL Server 2012. Used together in your queries, they allow you to extract a portion of rows from your result set.

We will look at typical SELECT query which you can run against the AdventureWorks database and add in ORDER BY clause.

```
SELECT BusinessEntityID, FirstName, MiddleName, LastName
FROM [Person].[Person]
ORDER BY BusinessEntityID
```

The following result set would be returned:

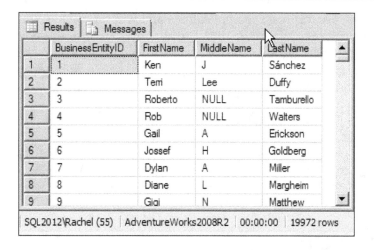

The query returns over 19,000 rows. However, what if you wanted to retrieve just a selection of rows from within that result set and using the SELECT TOP statement doesn't deliver the record you need? In comes the combination of OFFSET and FETCH. Take a look at the following query:

```
SELECT BusinessEntityID, FirstName, MiddleName, LastName
FROM [Person].[Person]
ORDER BY BusinessEntityID
OFFSET 100 ROWS
FETCH NEXT 5 ROWS ONLY
```

	BusinessEntityID	FirstName	MiddleName	LastName
1	101	Houman	N	Poumasseh
2	102	Zheng	W	Mu
3	103	Ebru	N	Ersan
4	104	Mary	R	Baker
5	105	Kevin	M	Homer

Here, the OFFSET tells the query to ignore the first 100 rows and then return only the following five rows. This is very easy to use and a quick way to return just a portion of records.

A great practical use for this is in applications and websites where you wish to display just a small selection of records. The advantage over traditional techniques is that all of the work is done on the server. This means that only those records the user is interested in viewing are transferred over the network, reducing bandwidth requirements and memory usage at the client application end.

You *must* remember your ORDER BY clause – this will affect which subsection of rows is returned using the OFFSET and FETCH combination. It is a common misconception that you can rely on a database engine to return rows in the order of the primary key. You can't, unless you specify an ORDER BY clause.

SEQUENCE

You are no doubt used to IDENTITY and how this works with a seed and increment value. SEQUENCE is structured in a very similar way, but with fewer limitations, giving it a welcome flexibility.

A SEQUENCE object is created at the database level but, unlike an IDENTITY property, it can be used across multiple tables. An IDENTITY value is generated when you insert a row into a table and it cannot be updated. You can retrieve the SEQUENCE value at any time and reset it without altering its previous value, and even set a minimum and maximum value. Let us look at a simple example:

```
CREATE SEQUENCE mySequence AS int
START WITH 1
INCREMENT BY 1
```

As you can see, mySequence is now available for use by all tables in the database:

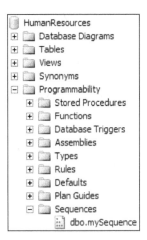

We have not used the SEQUENCE object yet, so the first value returned should be 1. Run the following statement to confirm this:

```
SELECT NEXT VALUE FOR mySequence AS [Next Value]
```

We can see that the SEQUENCE has not been used:

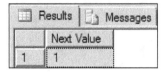

Next we will create a table so we can put SEQUENCEto the test. Run the following code to create the Employee table:

```
CREATE TABLE Employee
(
    EmployeeID int NOT NULL,
    FirstName varchar(30) NOT NULL,
    LastName varchar(30) NOT NULL
)
```

Now we will insert a couple of rows. Note that in the following code we use NEXT VALUE FOR just as we did in the preceding code to return the next SEQUENCE value. This will increment the SEQUENCE, in our case by one, though you can set this to be whatever you wish when you declare the SEQUENCE:

```
INSERT INTO Employee (EmployeeID, FirstName, LastName)
VALUES
(NEXT VALUE FOR mySequence, 'Rachel', 'Clements'),
(NEXT VALUE FOR mySequence, 'Jon', 'Reade')
GO

SELECT * FROM Employee
```

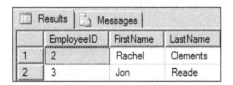

Our increment increases by one each time just as we would expect. If we re-run the following statement three times:

```
SELECT NEXT VALUE FOR mySequence AS [Next Value]
```

We can see that the sequence has incremented each time:

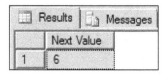

Now insert a couple more employees. If the NEXT VALUE FOR has not been run elsewhere, then the next value will start at 7:

```
INSERT INTO Employee (EmployeeID, FirstName, LastName)
VALUES
(NEXT VALUE FOR mySequence, 'Sam', 'Smith'),
(NEXT VALUE FOR mySequence, 'Jane', 'Jones')
GO

SELECT * FROM Employee
```

	EmployeeID	FirstName	LastName
1	2	Rachel	Clements
2	3	Jon	Reade
3	7	Sam	Smith
4	8	Jane	Jones

The SEQUENCE doesn't have to be unique; we can reset the seed to use the same value again. If we had a unique constraint on our EmployeeID column we would not be able to do this, but because we have not added a constraint, we can have some fun. Run the following statement:

```
ALTER SEQUENCE mySequence
RESTART WITH 1
```

This sets the SEQUENCE value back to 1 the next time it is retrieved. Add a couple more records to the table to see this in action:

```
INSERT INTO Employee (EmployeeID, FirstName, LastName)
VALUES
(NEXT VALUE FOR mySequence, 'John', 'Smith'),
(NEXT VALUE FOR mySequence, 'Simon', 'Jones')
```

```
GO

SELECT * FROM Employee
```

	EmployeeID	FirstName	LastName
1	2	Rachel	Clements
2	3	Jon	Reade
3	7	Sam	Smith
4	8	Jane	Jones
5	1	John	Smith
6	2	Simon	Jones

As you can see from the preceding screenshot, because we restarted the SEQUENCE, Rachel Clements and Simon Jones now have the same EmployeeID. You can reset the value by right-clicking on the SEQUENCE in the **Object Explorer** pane and choosing **Properties**. Check the **Restart sequence** box and click on the **OK** button:

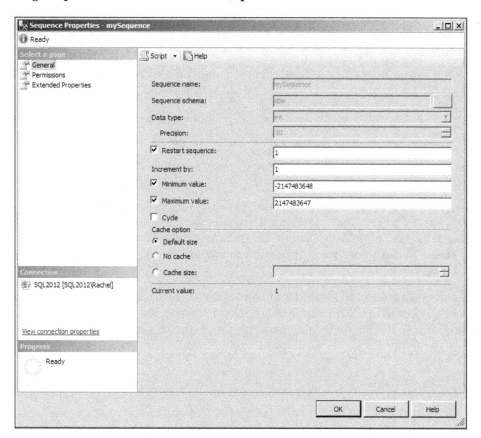

If we wanted to set a minimum and maximum value we could have declared our SEQUENCE as follows:

```
CREATE SEQUENCE mySequence AS int
START WITH 1
INCREMENT BY 1
MINVALUE 1
MAXVALUE 15
```

However we can change the maximum value using an ALTER statement. We shall set this maximum value to 10:

```
ALTER SEQUENCE mySequence
MAXVALUE 10
```

Run SELECT NEXT VALUE FOR mySequence AS [Next Value] until it reaches a value of 9:

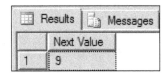

Now let us add in two rows which will take us past the MAXVALUE of 10 and see how SQL Server responds:

```
INSERT INTO Employee (EmployeeID, FirstName, LastName)
VALUES
(NEXT VALUE FOR mySequence, 'Chris', 'Doe'),
(NEXT VALUE FOR mySequence, 'Robert', 'Smith')
```

We receive the following error:

```
Msg 11728, Level 16, State 1, Line 1
The sequence object 'mySequence' has reached its minimum or
maximum value. Restart the sequence object to allow new values
to be generated.
```

If we wanted to restrict the number of rows inserted into a table we could use a SEQUENCE object to limit this number. So as you can see, the seed and increment values operate in the same fashion as IDENTITY, but you are free to use and manipulate it.

WITH RESULT SETS

The EXECUTE statement has been extended in SQL Server 2012 to include the WITH RESULT SETS option. This allows you to change the column names and data types of the result set returned in the execution of a stored procedure.

We will jump straight into an example to see how this works. The following procedure returns a straightforward result set using the Employee table we created in the previous section:

```
CREATE PROC spGet_Employees
AS
SELECT EmployeeID, FirstName, LastName
FROM Employee
ORDER BY EmployeeID
```

If we call this stored procedure in the usual way it will return all columns. The data type of each column will be the same as the column type in the table.

```
EXEC spGet_Employees
```

In the previous section, we used the mySequence SEQUENCE object to set the value that was inserted into the EmployeeID column. We want to return the result set so the integer EmployeeID column is a varchar instead. To see how you can easily change the name of the columns, we will output EmployeeID as NI_Number and LastName as Surname. We can do this easily using WITH RESULT SETS:

```
EXEC spGet_Employees
WITH RESULT SETS
(
    (
    NI_Number varchar(15),
    FirstName varchar(30),
    Surname varchar(30)
    )
)
```

	NI_Number	FirstName	Surname
1	1	John	Smith
2	2	Simon	Jones
3	2	Rachel	Clements
4	3	Jon	Reade
5	7	Sam	Smith
6	8	Jane	Jones

This is an easy and flexible option for executing a stored procedure and transforming the result set to be in the format you need.

Error handling with THROW

The TRY... CATCH error handling construct is very similar in T-SQL to exception handling in languages such as C# or VB.NET. In T-SQL it consists of a TRY block and a CATCH block, which must always be paired. If an error occurs in the TRY block, it is passed to the CATCH block code to handle.

In previous versions of SQL Server you would use @@RAISE_ERROR and would need to neatly collect the error data and return this. Let us look at an example that will throw an error:

```
BEGIN TRY
   DECLARE @MyInt int
   SET @MyInt = 1 / 0
END TRY
BEGIN CATCH
   DECLARE @ErrorMessage nvarchar(4000), @ErrorSeverity int
   SELECT @ErrorMessage = ERROR_MESSAGE(),
   @ErrorSeverity = ERROR_SEVERITY()
   RAISERROR (@ErrorMessage, @ErrorSeverity, 1)
END CATCH
```

This is the result:

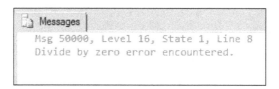

```
Messages
   Msg 50000, Level 16, State 1, Line 8
   Divide by zero error encountered.
```

In the preceding CATCH block, there is a lot of work going on to collect the details of this error. Now there is a slicker way of finding out what has caused the error. Compare the above code to the code below:

```
BEGIN TRY
   DECLARE @MyInt int
   SET @MyInt = 1/0
END TRY
   BEGIN CATCH
   -- throw out the error
THROW
END CATCH
```

Look at the error message output:

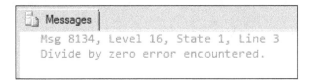

You can still write custom errors for your T-SQL, but it is worth using THROW as this one word can tell you just as much, with less effort.

 It takes some doing to write error-free code, especially when things that are out of your immediate control can change and break your code. TRY... CATCH blocks handle any errors in your code with grace, so if you have not yet adopted this construct, it can become a real friend!

FileTable table type

FileTable is a new type of table which builds on the existing FILESTREAM functionality that was introduced in SQL Server 2008. FILESTREAM is an efficient way to store documents inside the database, as they are managed by SQL Server and included in any backups. You can store any type of file and up to any size—the only limit is the size of the disk the FILESTREAM store sits on.

FILESTREAM effectively manages the files you insert, whereas FileTable will allow access through Windows to the properties of files stored on the NT file system. In effect, FileTable really is a table of files. This is where it becomes exciting, as you are about to discover.

 SQL Server FILESTREAM makes file handling efficient and secure. To read more about how it works and how to configure your server (it is really easy to do), see Paul Randal's White Paper:http://msdn. microsoft.com/en-us/library/cc949109.aspx

You can add files to the table without having to use the FILESTREAM method of creating a transactional context and streaming into the table. Furthermore, it will store the size and type of the file, along with data such as date created, last modified date, and other attributes. This data can be used for full-text searches too.

Next, we will create a database with FILESTREAM functionality so we can add a FileTable table. This code assumes you have already configured your server for FILESTREAM:

```
CREATE DATABASE Documents
ON PRIMARY
(
    NAME = N'Documents',
    FILENAME = N'C:\SQL2012\Documents.mdf'
),
FILEGROUPFSGROUP CONTAINS FILESTREAM
(
    NAME = FSData,
    FILENAME= 'C:\SQL2012\FSDataStore.ndf'
)
LOG ON
(
    NAME = N'Documents_Log',
    FILENAME = N'C:\SQL2012\Documents_log.ldf'
)
WITH FILESTREAM
(
    NON_TRANSACTED_ACCESS = FULL,
    DIRECTORY_NAME = N'Documents'
)
```

Now that we have created our database, we will add a new FileTable table called DocumentStore:

```
CREATE TABLE DocumentStore AS FileTable
WITH
(
    FileTable_Directory = 'DocumentStore',
    FileTable_Collate_Filename = database_default
)
```

If you refresh your database list in SSMS, you will see your new database. Expand the **Tables** node and there is a folder called **FileTables**. Under here is the **DocumentStore** table. Expand the table node to see the full column list:

```
□ 🗎 Documents
   ⊞ 📁 Database Diagrams
   □ 📁 Tables
      ⊞ 📁 System Tables
      □ 📁 FileTables
         □ 🗎 dbo.DocumentStore
            □ 📁 Columns
               🗎 stream_id (uniqueidentifier, not null)
               🗎 file_stream (varbinary(max), null)
               🗎 name (nvarchar(255), not null)
               🔑 path_locator (PK, hierarchyid, not null)
               🔑 parent_path_locator (FK, Computed, hierarchyid, null)
               🗎 file_type (Computed, nvarchar(255), null)
               🗎 cached_file_size (Computed, bigint, null)
               🗎 creation_time (datetimeoffset(7), not null)
               🗎 last_write_time (datetimeoffset(7), not null)
               🗎 last_access_time (datetimeoffset(7), null)
               🗎 is_directory (bit, not null)
               🗎 is_offline (bit, not null)
               🗎 is_hidden (bit, not null)
               🗎 is_readonly (bit, not null)
               🗎 is_archive (bit, not null)
               🗎 is_system (bit, not null)
               🗎 is_temporary (bit, not null)
            ⊞ 📁 Keys
            ⊞ 📁 Constraints
            ⊞ 📁 Triggers
            ⊞ 📁 Indexes
```

We have not yet added any documents, so we will do that next. Right click on the newly created `FileTable`, in our case **DocumentStore**, to open the menu and choose **Explore FileTable Directory**.

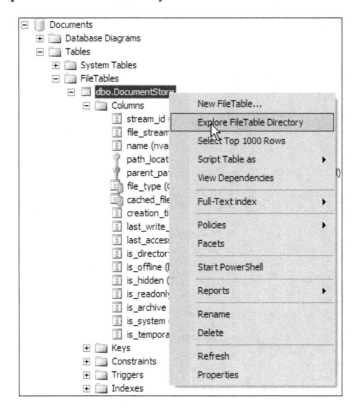

This will open a **Windows Explorer** window, which will be empty as nothing is in there yet. Drag in some files, just as you would to any other file location and return to SSMS.

You can now query the `FileTable` to see the documents you have just added:

```
SELECT [name], file_type, cached_file_size, last_access_time,
       is_readonly
FROM DocumentStore
```

This now shows us the attributes of the files we have just added and they can be queried from any application:

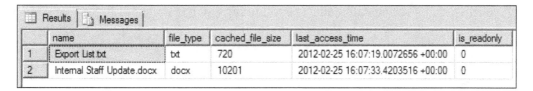

	name	file_type	cached_file_size	last_access_time	is_readonly
1	Export List.txt	txt	720	2012-02-25 16:07:19.0072656 +00:00	0
2	Internal Staff Update.docx	docx	10201	2012-02-25 16:07:33.4203516 +00:00	0

This is an incredibly powerful feature as it allows you to use an application to publicize the metadata for any documents you store in the `FileTable` data type, without having direct access to the Windows file system. The real beauty is in the ease and speed with which it can be set up and used.

> To find out about the `FileTable` prerequisites, bulk loading files, and using the File I/O APIs, please read through the documentation on the Microsoft site: `http://msdn.microsoft.com/en-us/library/ff929144(v=sql.110).aspx`

New T-SQL analytical functions

Transact SQL now includes some great new analytical functions, similar to those that exist in MDX. Rather than taking a hard-to-understand dataset from the `AdventureWorks` database, let us create a simple one of our own to understand what some of the most useful functions do:

```
CREATE TABLE Sales
(
    SalesYear int,
    SalesAmount int
)

INSERT    INTO Sales
VALUES    (2000, 100),
          (2001, 250),
          (2002, 300),
          (2003, 400),
          (2004, 375)
```

Let us run a quick select statement. The following is what we should see:

	SalesYear	SalesAmount
1	2000	100
2	2001	250
3	2002	300
4	2003	400
5	2004	375

Now we will use some of the new functions.

FIRST_VALUE

This function, as its name suggests, returns the first value from an ordered set of values. This is really useful as we can calculate, inside a result set, the difference between an initial value and each subsequent value on-the-fly. With no variables and no re-querying, everything is done inside a single piece of Transact SQL:

```
SELECT    SalesYear,
          SalesAmount,
          FIRST_VALUE (SalesAmount)
OVER (ORDER BY SalesAmount) AS FirstYearSales,
          SalesAmount - FIRST_VALUE (SalesAmount)
OVER (ORDER BY SalesAmount) AS SalesGrowthSinceFirstYear
FROM      Sales
ORDER     BY SalesYear
```

Running this query will return the following result set:

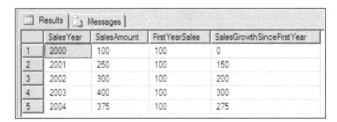

	SalesYear	SalesAmount	FirstYearSales	SalesGrowthSinceFirstYear
1	2000	100	100	0
2	2001	250	100	150
3	2002	300	100	200
4	2003	400	100	300
5	2004	375	100	275

LAST_VALUE

This is the opposite of FIRST_VALUE and it returns the last value from an ordered set of values.

LAG

LAG allows you to access a value in the previous (lagging) row, without joining
a result set to itself. This is really helpful in comparing sales from previous years,
or a server state compared to its previous value:

```
SELECT SalesYear, SalesAmount, LAG(SalesAmount,1,0)
OVER (ORDER BY SalesYear) AS PreviousYearSalesAmount,
        SalesAmount - LAG(SalesAmount,1,0)
OVER (ORDER BY SalesYear) AS YearOnYearDifference
FROM Sales
```

	SalesYear	SalesAmount	PreviousYearSalesAmount	YearOnYearDifference
1	2000	100	0	100
2	2001	250	100	150
3	2002	300	250	50
4	2003	400	300	100
5	2004	375	400	-25

LEAD

The opposite of LAG, LEAD gives you the value from a column in the next row of
an ordered data set.

SQL Server Data Tools

Depending on the scope of your development role, you may find that you use more
than one version of Visual Studio: Visual Studio 2010 for creating and managing
your database projects and Visual Studio 2008, or Business Intelligence Development
Studio (BIDS) for your BI projects (SSIS, SSAS and SSRS). In the past, the SQL Server
development toolset has lagged behind, remaining on an older version of Microsoft's
development environment, but it has finally caught up.

SQL Server 2012 says goodbye to BIDS and introduces us to SQL Server Data Tools
(SSDT). Based on the Visual Studio 2010 shell, SSDT thankfully brings everything
under the same roof. If you already use Visual Studio 2010 for software or web
applications, then you are in the same familiar environment.

Just like BIDS, SSDT is a free tool available to all SQL Server developers as part
of the standard SQL Server installation options, so you don't need to have Visual
Studio 2010 already installed. But if you do, you can download add-ins to extend
your toolset. This is good news for developers.

It is worth noting that SSDT is not a replacement for SQL Server Management Studio (SSMS). SSMS is still your single application for managing and administering SQL Server, and of course you can still develop using SSMS if you wish.

Database Projects

SSDT supports the ability to create database projects. If you are not already using database projects to manage your objects, we recommend you do, because there are so many advantages. For starters, a database project allows you to use source control to handle changes, which is critical whatever you are developing and especially for team development. Your database project is deployed to the server as a whole by creating a script which manages all the changes for you. This saves developers from randomly executing ALTER statements or waiting on the DBA to run them on their behalf, so the whole database can be updated in one operation. Furthermore, because you build your project in advance, you can check for errors upfront, making for a slick and safe deployment.

Database projects make it very easy to keep your development and production databases identical, as you only have one version to deploy. You can deploy to as many servers as you wish, instantly creating an empty copy of the database.

Whether you are a developer or DBA, we highly recommend you use database projects. Once you have tried one, we reckon you won't go back to using SSMS to create and alter your scripts.

Support for SQL Server 2005, 2008 and SQL Azure

This is fantastic news. SQL Server Data Tools supports connections to all versions and editions of SQL Server from SQL Server 2005 onwards. Most organizations run a mix of versions, so this is really helpful to us as developers. Furthermore this is your new development platform for SQL Azure.

IntelliSense and debugging

You will use SSDT for creating tables, views, triggers, stored procedures, and all the usual objects that comprise a typical database schema. Full T-SQL IntelliSense is included in the toolset and works well. IntelliSense in previous versions of Management Studio has often been unresponsive and disappointing, but inside SSDT, as with Visual Studio 2010, this is much improved.

You can execute queries and debug your code inside SSDT, making full use of break points and the ability to step through your code inside stored procedures too. This will really boost your development productivity.

Installing SQL Server Data Tools

If you remember back in *Chapter 1, Installing SQL Server 2012,* when we installed SQL Server, we had the option to include SQL Server Data Tools as one of the included features. If you installed SQL Server on your dedicated database server, the chances are that you didn't install SSDT. However you will need it on the machine you are developing on. Your operating system version will need to be at a minimum Windows Vista SP2, Windows 7 SP1, or Windows Server 2008 SP2, or Windows Server 2008 SP1 (or any higher version of these).

Installing without Visual Studio 2010 pre-installed

If you have not already got a copy of the Visual Studio 2010 IDE shell installed, then you can install it from the SQL Server installation media, or download it from the Microsoft site (refer to the next link). To install it from the SQL Server media, run the setup file until you reach the **Feature Selection** screen and under the list of **Shared Features**, put a tick in the **SQL Server Data Tools** checkbox. Follow the installation instructions to the end.

By installing it this way, this includes the add-ins you need to create SSIS, SSAS and SSRS projects.

Installing with Visual Studio 2010 pre-installed

If you already have Visual Studio 2010 installed, check to ensure that you have applied SP1. If not, use the link in the following information box to download and apply this service pack. Then you can download SQL Server Data Tools. Follow the installation instructions to give the Visual Studio 2010 shell SQL Server Data Tools capability.

 To acquire Visual Studio 2010 and the SQL Server Data Tools, point your browser at http://msdn.microsoft.com/en-us/data/tools.aspx. Here you will find a link for Visual Studio 2010 SP1 and some tips to help you start using it.

Creating a new project

If you installed Visual Studio 2010 on its own, go to **Start | Programs | Microsoft Visual Studio 2010**. If you installed it from the SQL Server media installation, you will probably find that it is also listed as **SQL Server Data Tools** under the **Microsoft SQL Server 2012** folder on your program menu:

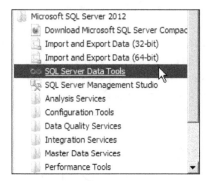

Furthermore, it will be listed as Microsoft Visual Studio 2010, but they are the same tool. When you have opened SSDT for the first time, you will see the following screen:

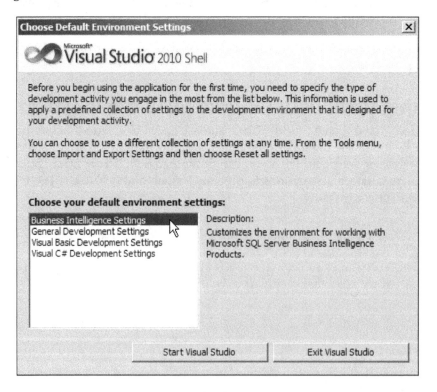

We will choose the **Business Intelligence Settings** option in this case, as we want to create BI projects. Make your selection and then click on the **Start Visual Studio** button. The first time this runs, it takes a minute or so to configure your environment to these settings. As soon as it is complete, you will see the Visual Studio Start Page. Click on the **New Project** icon on the **Start Page**, or go to **File | New | Project**. Both methods will open the **New Project** dialog box:

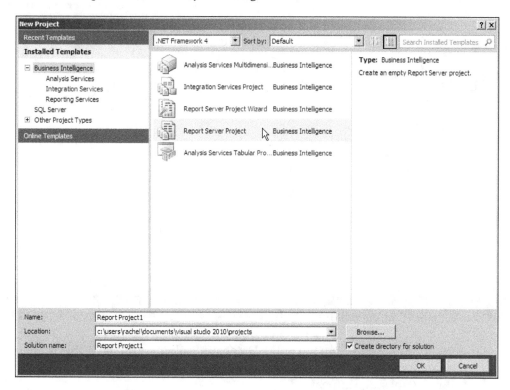

As you can see from the **Installed Templates**, you can now choose a project template for **Analysis Services**, **Integration Services** or **Reporting Services**.

Creating database projects

If you are already using Visual Studio 2010 for your database projects, you will be familiar with the benefits of creating and deploying your schemas to the server.

From **SQL Server Data Tools**:

1. Open the **New Project** dialog box
2. Under **Installed Templates**, click on **SQL Server**.

3. In the centre pane, you will notice the available list of project templates change and will see something similar to the following screenshot:

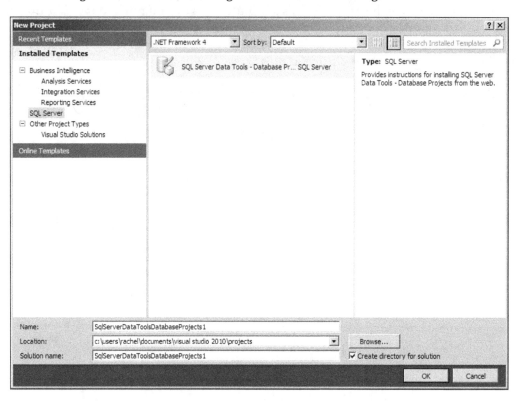

As you can see, we have the SSDT Database Project template. If this is the first time you have chosen this project type, you will see the following message appear:

4. You need to install a separate component to create database projects. Go ahead and click on the **Install** button. This will open your default browser and take you to the page on the Microsoft site, as listed previously. Click on the link to download SQL Server Data Tools and the web installer will run. Follow the download and installation instructions and this will add the capability to allow you to create database projects in SSDT:

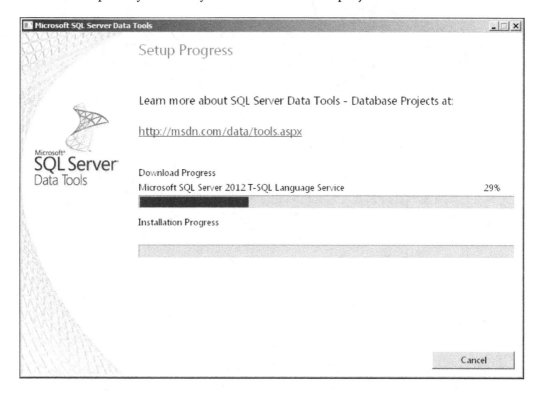

5. Once you have installed the extra tools, open SSDT and you will see the screen to set up your environment, this time offering you **SQL Server Development Settings**:

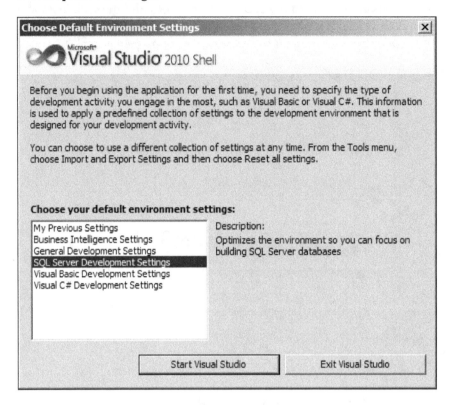

6. You can choose **My Previous Settings** to leave the environment as it was before, but whatever you decide, this won't make so much of a difference that it will affect your various development projects, be it a VB.NET, database, or SSRS project.

7. Open the **New Project** dialog box once more and you will see the **SQL Server Database Project** listed under the SQL Server template. You can now create a database project.

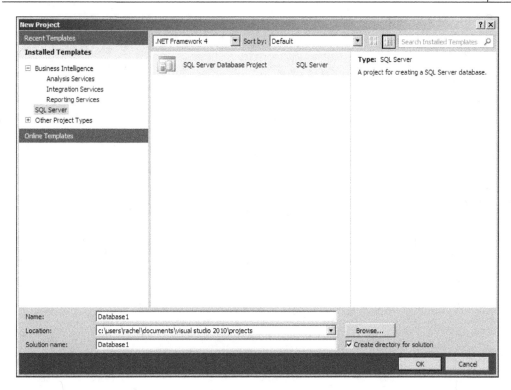

Summary

In this chapter, we looked at T-SQL's new CONCAT and FORMAT functions. We saw how OFFSET and FETCH allow you access to just one block of your result set and how SEQUENCE can give you the functionality of IDENTITY but take it to a whole new level. Then we saw how TRY CATCH blocks have been improved to allow simpler, neater error handling. After that we looked at an example of how to use the handy new FileTable table to access the underlying file system.

These are useful and welcome additions to Transact SQL and we recommend you familiarize yourself with them and add them to your toolkit of programming skills. They are advantageous to have at hand and we are confident they will soon become a major part of your everyday programming use.

Finally, we looked at SQL Server Data Tools, which replaces the well-loved BIDS development environment and works across all versions of SQL Server from 2005 onwards.

In the next chapter we will be looking at the new features in Analysis Services, which follows on from the analytical functions we have just seen.

4
Analysis Services

In this chapter we will be focusing on the new features that catapult both SQL Server and Analysis Services straight into the 21st century. Some of these features we have not touched upon, particularly surrounding the advances in PowerPivot and SharePoint. These are specialist topics, and are big enough to demand a book of their own.

When we first read about the new Analysis Services features, one of the first things that immediately came to our attention was the new tabular architecture model. There are now three models to choose from when configuring SQL Sever Analysis Services, so we will explore all three to help you understand which one you need. We will examine how to set up the three models, how to find out which one is running and how to change the model.

You will learn how to override the string store limit of 4 GB and upgrade projects from earlier versions of SQL Server to take advantage of this new storage capability.

We found this chapter particularly interesting and exciting to write and hope you enjoy it too, so let's get started!

Business Intelligence Semantic Model

What does Microsoft imply when talking about the **Business Intelligence Semantic Model (BISM)**? Fundamentally, it is the Analysis Services storage engine in which you choose to store your analytical data. The solution may also include SharePoint, Reporting Services, Excel or a custom BI application.

SQL Server 2012 Analysis Services introduces a new Business Intelligence Semantic Model called tabular modeling. We will take a look at what this new model offers, as well as exploring the two existing models and how xVelocity fits in.

While we refer to these as "models", as does Microsoft in their documentation, it can be helpful to think of them as different types of Analysis Services storage engines. We recommend reading Analysis Services expert Chris Webb's excellent article "So, what is the BI Semantic Model?" at `http://cwebbbi.wordpress.com/2012/02/14/so-what-is-the-bi-semantic-model`.

The three models

Whether you are a BI developer or the DBA charged with keeping Analysis Services up and running, you need to know about the three different server models. These models determine the types of solutions that can be delivered in your organization.

The three models are **Multidimensional and data mining** (the default model), **Tabular**, and **PowerPivot for SharePoint**. You can only run one model per instance. If you need more than one, you can run all three models as separate instances on the same server, if you so wish. If you later find that you have installed the wrong model, you can uninstall it and re-install another. The three models function in different ways and we will explore each model in the upcoming section.

> Check with your business users and developers before starting your Analysis Services installation to see if there are particular features they need, and ensure they are included in the model you plan to provide. For a side-by-side comparison across the three models, check out the model features' matrix at:
>
> `http://msdn.microsoft.com/en-us/library/hh212940(v=sql.110).aspx`.

Multidimensional and data mining model

This is the default model and it will run multidimensional databases and data mining models. If you have been using a previous version of Analysis Services, then you will be familiar with this model. Use this model if your solution uses cubes to analyze data across dimensions.

The biggest advantage of building a multidimensional model in Analysis Services is the speedy performance of ad hoc queries against the data. You or your BI developers can create cubes that respond quickly and offer a single source of data for reporting. It is easy to integrate with Reporting Services and Excel, as well as third-party and custom applications, which makes it an attractive BI solution.

Creating a multidimensional model database

An Analysis Services database comprises data sources, data source views, cubes and dimensions. It may also have data mining structures and user-defined functions. To create a database, deploy your Analysis Services project from **SQL Server Data Tools (SSDT)** to an instance of Analysis Services. This process will create an Analysis Services database (if it doesn't already exist) and instantiate the objects within the database. Changes are only applied on the server when you deploy the project.

The alternative method is to create an empty database in Management Studio or SSDT and then connect to the database using SSDT to create objects within it, rather than inside a project. In this case, any changes are effective as soon as you save them.

Tabular model

We think the new tabular model is likely to be widely adopted. If you have a relational database background (like us), you will probably like Analysis Services tabular model databases, as they are a lot easier to build. However, administrative tasks are still similar to those required for the SSAS multidimensional model, as a tabular model database runs within the Analysis Services engine.

The tabular model is easier to grasp conceptually for developers who have only developed in a relational environment and it is easier to deploy tabular models. In addition, it can be used in `DirectQuery` mode to reduce the duplication of data inherent in traditional OLAP and the `Cached` mode tabular implementations, which we will explore later on.

Tabular model database

Put simply, a tabular database is an in-memory database. It stores data in a more table-like manner that is similar to relational tables, rather than in multidimensional facts and dimensions, or cubes. Tabular model databases exist inside Analysis Services and are accessed through the xVelocity database engine, which is an alternative to the multidimensional Analysis Services engine (that has been around for the last decade). Note that the xVelocity database engine does not replace the Analysis Services engine; it just provides an alternative for those who are not so familiar with the multidimensional way of doing things.

The xVelocity engine is used because it provides cutting-edge data compression alongside a multithreaded query processor. Together, these give xVelocity-based databases their blisteringly fast speed and allow large databases to be easily contained within server memory, without fetching from, or updating data to, much slower disk storage.

To use Analysis Services with the *xVelocity* engine, you need to install it in the new tabular engine mode. This model lets you run tabular databases on your Analysis Server instances.

The xVelocity tabular engine mode

The xVelocity tabular engine supports two modes for tabular databases — the Cached mode and the DirectQuery mode. So what is the difference? Cached mode pulls data in from relational data sources and/or flat files, caching it in memory. In contrast, the DirectQuery mode completely bypasses the in-memory model and queries the data directly from the relational source.

If you are an experienced DBA, you may have just flinched while reading that last sentence. Querying directly against your relational source will have an impact on the server resources and affect performance. If you decide to use this mode, be careful where and when you use it. If you can copy the data to a replica database on a dedicated server, this would be a good option to avoid the potential load on your production system.

Each of the models has its advantages and disadvantages. A limitation of the tabular model's default Cached mode is that when the source data changes, data is not refreshed. This means that the results may be out of date as changes to the underlying data will not be reflected in the query. In addition, when a system hosting the Cached mode model is shut down, the cache is saved to disk and has to be reloaded when the model is next opened, which can take time. Finally, it is more difficult to ensure that data is secured in the same way as it is on the source system.

 A full discussion of DirectQuery mode can be found at: http://msdn.microsoft.com/en-us/library/hh230898.

Creating a tabular model database

You create a tabular model database in the SQL Server Data Tools application using a tabular model project template. Create a new project and then choose **Analysis Services Tabular Project**:

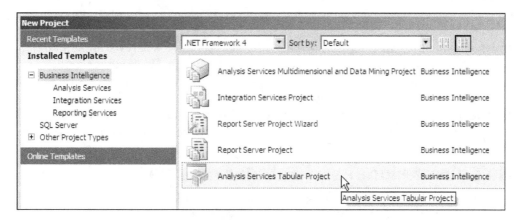

You can create the data sources, add columns and relationships between them, and deploy the model to an Analysis Services instance, all from within one tool.

Microsoft has created a really good tutorial to walk you through the creation of a tabular model project. Among other things, it will show you how to add data and create relationships, as well as calculate columns, measures and key performance indicators. Kick-start your learning by pointing your browser at:

`http://msdn.microsoft.com/en-us/library/hh231691.aspx.`

PowerPivot for the SharePoint model

The PowerPivot model was available in SQL Server 2008 R2 for SharePoint installations. It is an in-memory database that extends SharePoint 2010 and Excel Services by adding server-side processing, as well as document management for PowerPivot workbooks, which are published to SharePoint.

PowerPivot workbooks are Excel Workbook files (`.xlsx`) containing potentially large, related datasets that are built in a PowerPivot add-in window inside Excel, using PivotTables and PivotCharts in a worksheet. The PowerPivot server components deliver the server-side query processing of the PowerPivot data that users then access from SharePoint.

Microsoft has provided a short, useful guide to upgrading an existing PowerPivot for SharePoint installation from SQL Server 2008 R2 to SQL Server 2012 at: `http://msdn.microsoft.com/en-us/library/hh230964.aspx.`

Installing a model

You may remember in *Chapter 1, Installing SQL Server 2012* when we looked at the SQL Server installation steps, which you can set up the SSAS Server mode during the installation process. If you didn't choose to install SSAS at the same time you installed the database engine, you can go back and add this by running the installation setup file again. The multidimensional and tabular models are set up in a very similar way; PowerPivot is somewhat different as it requires SharePoint.

Multidimensional and Tabular models

Run your SQL Server setup process as a new installation, or choose to add features if you didn't initially install Analysis Services. Make sure you add Analysis Services to the list of features to install. Follow the installation screens as per *Chapter 1, Installing SQL Server 2012* until you reach the **Analysis Services Configuration** screen. You will see on the **Server Configuration** tab that the **Server Mode** option is defaulted to **Multidimensional and Data Mining Mode**. Select this or **Tabular Mode** depending on which one you need:

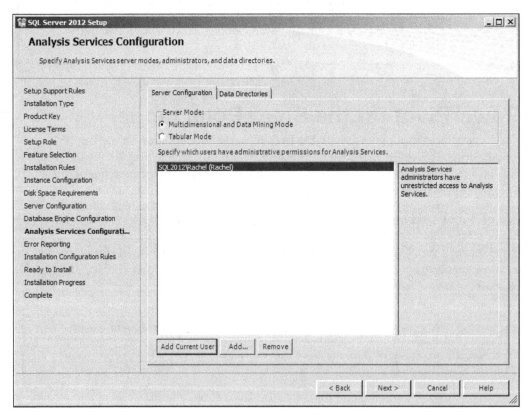

Click on the **Add Current User** button and add yourself to the list of Analysis Services administrators. Click on **Next** and continue with the rest of the installation. Refer to *Chapter 1, Installing SQL Server 2012* if you need further instructions on completing the installation.

PowerPivot for SharePoint

To install PowerPivot for SharePoint, follow these steps:

1. Run the SQL Server 2012 setup file on the same server.
2. Choose the first option, **New SQL Server stand-alone installation or add features to an existing installation**.
3. Navigate through to the **Setup Role** screen.
4. Select **SQL Server PowerPivot for SharePoint**. Note the checkbox option **Add SQL Server Database Relational Engine Services to this installation**. This is useful if you are setting up a new SharePoint farm and want to manage configurations and databases. This installs a PowerPivot named instance, as shown in the following screenshot:

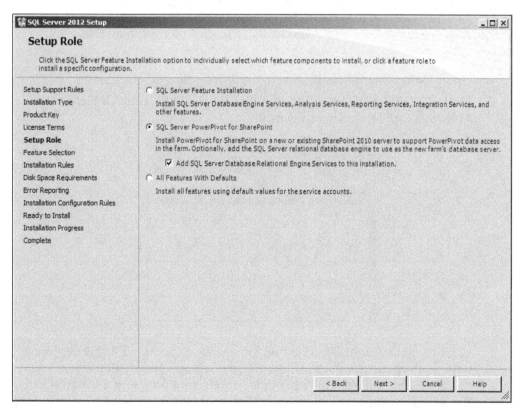

5. Click on **Next** and follow the rest of the set up screens through to the **Installation Progress** option.

To take advantage of the new features in SQL Server 2012, you will need to install SharePoint Server 2010 SP1 before you configure PowerPivot.

> For full instructions on setting up SharePoint and SQL Server PowerPivot, follow the step-by-step instructions on the Microsoft site at:
> `http://msdn.microsoft.com/en-us/library/`
> `ee210708(v=sql.110).aspx`

Determining a previously installed model

It may be the case that you didn't install Analysis Services, or indeed are unsure which model you chose during the setup. There are two ways of finding out which version is running on an instance: you can open SSMS and look at the icon used for Analysis Services, or look at the `DeploymentMode` property in the `INI` file that was created during the installation.

The quickest way is to open SSMS and look at the icon, so we can do that using the following steps:

1. Open **Management Studio**.

2. From the **Object Explorer**, choose **Connect** and then **Analysis Services**, as shown in the following screenshot:

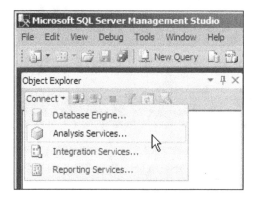

3. Log in to your Analysis Server and look at the icon in the **Object Explorer** pane. As you can see in the following screenshot, our default instance uses the multidimensional and data mining model and our named instance uses the tabular model:

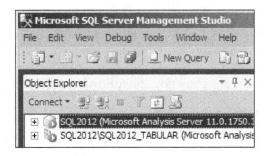

The slightly longer, though perhaps more reliable route (should Microsoft ever change the icons) is to open the msmdserv.ini file using the following steps and see what the value is:

1. To locate the file, right-click on the **Analysis Server** node in **Management Studio** to bring up the menu.

2. Choose **Properties**, as shown in the following screenshot:

3. This opens the **Analysis Server Properties** window. Look at the **DataDir** column and note the value in the right-hand column. This tells you where your installation files are located. In our case, we installed to the default folder on our c: drive. **MSAS11** shows us that this version number refers to SQL Server 2012, as shown in the following screenshot:

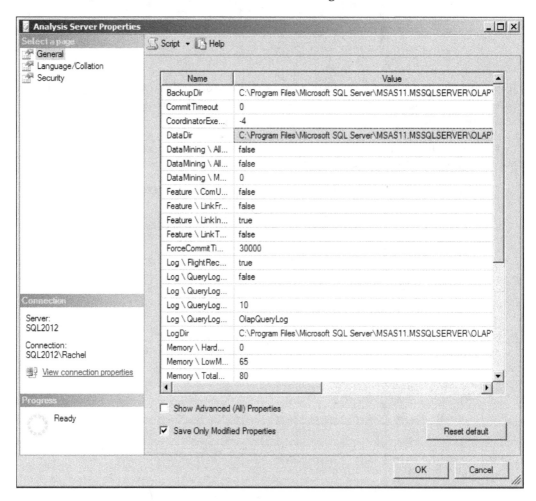

4. You can copy the value of the file directory structure, paste this into **Windows Explorer** and this will show you the msmdsrv.ini file, as you can see in the following screenshot:

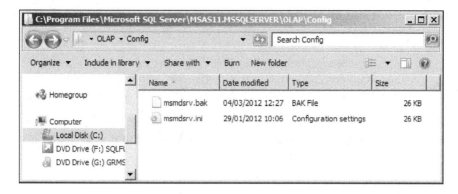

5. Right-click to open the file in Notepad and you will see plenty of XML code. Navigate to the `DeploymentMode` property and there you will find a value of **0** (Multidimensional), **1** (PowerPivot), or **2** (Tabular), as shown in the following screenshot:

As you can see, our installation shows **0**, or multidimensional.

Do not change the value in this file! This is not a supported way of changing your Analysis Services model. You will need to uninstall the current node, or install another instance to change the model.

If you are unable to gain access to this file, check to ensure that your SQL Server login is part of the Server Admin group.

Resource usage reporting

We are big fans of performance monitoring and always happy when Microsoft add new features to enhance the utilities that already exist. SQL Server 2012 introduces the `Resource Usage` event class. This new event class allows you to gather statistics on how your resources are used when processing queries.

Of course, there already are some useful DMVs that allow us to look at resource usage in Analysis Services. There is a great article here to begin with:

`http://dwbi1.wordpress.com/2010/01/01/ssas-dmv-dynamic-management-view`

You can monitor these events using SQL Server Profiler, just as you would with your OLTP systems. SQL Server Profiler monitors the engine process events such as logins, transactions starting and stopping, and what T-SQL code is executed on the server. It captures data about these events, such as how long it took to run, so you can track both server and database events.

Using SQL Server Profiler, you can monitor the overall performance of Analysis Services, debug **multidimensional expressions (MDX)**, find slow-running MDX statements, and step through your statements while in development.

Use SQL Server Profiler to capture events on your production server and save them to a file. You can then replay these events on your development or test servers to find any problems, without affecting users on your production system.

Next we will take a look at how to monitor Analysis Services. This process is the same for all the analysis engines; it is the events you monitor that will differ. Perform the following steps to use SQL Server Profiler:

1. From your **Program** menu, go to the **Microsoft SQL Server 2012** group and find the **Performance Tools** folder.

2. Click on **SQL Server Profiler**. This opens up SQL Server Profiler's empty environment.

3. From the **File** menu, choose **New Trace**. The **Connect to SQL Server** dialog window is opened.

4. In the **Server type** drop-down list, choose **Analysis Services**, as shown in the following screenshot:

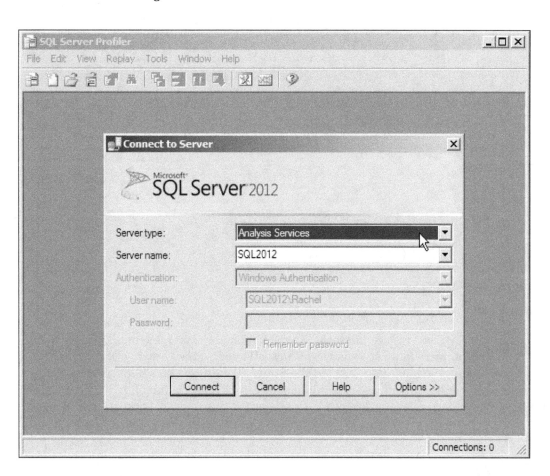

5. Select your server in the **Server name** drop-down, then click on **Connect**. This opens the **Trace Properties** dialog window. As shown in the following screenshot, we are saving our trace to both a file (.trc) and a table. We have a database called PerformanceMonitoring to store our trace data, and in this case, we will be monitoring our Products database and saving the data to the Trace_Products_DB table.

6. If you want your trace to end on a particular date and time, select the **Enable trace stop time** checkbox and enter your end date and time, as shown in the following screenshot:

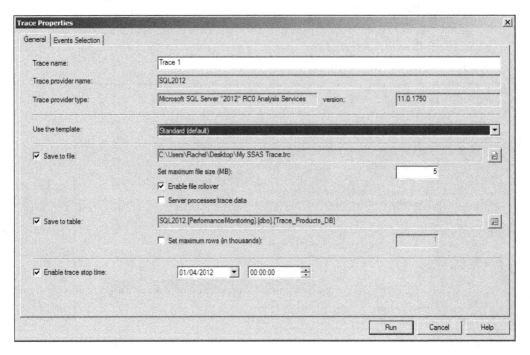

7. Now switch to the **Events Selection** tab.

8. In this case, we are interested in the Resource Usage events. They are not listed by default, so select the **Show all events** checkbox to bring up this event. We have also selected the **Show all columns** checkbox as we want to monitor all the data for this event, as can be seen in the following screenshot:

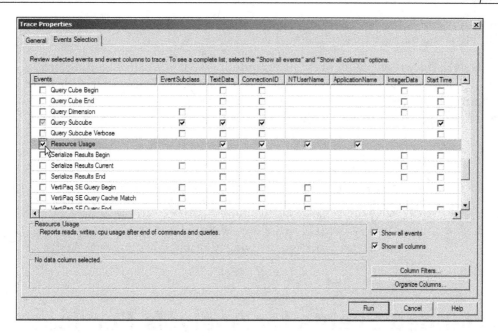

9. Uncheck the events and columns you don't want to gather data on and then click **Run**. This starts the trace and you can begin monitoring, as shown in the following screenshot:

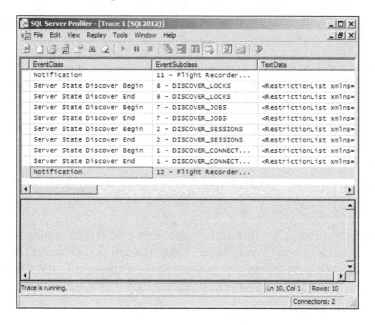

There is not much activity running on our server just yet, but as soon as we start running some queries, this will fill up.

Analysis Services has plenty of events to monitor, so it is worth spending time getting to know what is available. These events can really help you troubleshoot performance issues as well as tuning up queries. We recommend you bookmark the following page as it lists all Query Processing Events for Analysis Services:

`http://msdn.microsoft.com/en-us/library/hh272559(v=sql.110).aspx.`

 If you are running traces over a long period of time, don't forget about performance. By monitoring too many events, you will add load to the system, so only monitor the events you need. This also stops the trace file or the table where you are storing the events from becoming too big. You can also set a row limit if saving to a table, which prevents it from becoming too large.

Extended Events for Analysis Services

This is a geeky topic, even for this book. Nevertheless, if you develop event tracing for Analysis Services or, develop system monitoring tools, it is worth knowing that you can now trace Analysis Services using SQL Server's Extended Events framework. This event driven framework places little demand on resources, and is easily configured and scaled, handling and routing events from the database engine to consumer applications.

An entire book could be written on this subject as it is very specialized, so rather than wasting valuable space here by giving it perfunctory treatment or just repeating what has been said, we would recommend the following resources:

- Jonathan Kehayias and Bob Beauchemin have both talked at length about Extended Events at the UK SQL Server conference SQLBits. You can watch their videos at `http://sqlbits.com/Sessions/Event7/opening_the_sql_server_2008_toolbox_-_an_introduction_to_extended_events` and `http://sqlbits.com/Sessions/Event10/Extended_Events_and_the_new_Profiler_in_SQL_Server_2012`.

- An excellent blog site authored by the team that built Extended Events can be found at `http://blogs.msdn.com/b/extended_events`. This discusses intricacies for developers, such as using the **Extended Event Object Model**.

- BOL also covers Extended Event architecture and usage, and can be found at `http://msdn.microsoft.com/en-us/library/bb630282%28v=sql.110%29.aspx`.

- A list of Analysis Services trace events can be found at `http://msdn.microsoft.com/en-us/library/ms174867`.

 All Analysis Services events can be captured and targeted to specific consumers, as defined in SQL Server Extended Events, through XEvents. See MSDN at `http://msdn.microsoft.com/en-us/library/gg492139%28v=sql.110%29.aspx` for full details.

String store constraint

If you have ever encountered the error message File system error: a FileStore error from WriteFile occurred, then you will probably be all too familiar with the reason for this message. In a multidimensional database, strings are stored using a different architecture to numeric data so that performance optimizations can be made based on data characteristics.

A dimension attribute such as a name or location could be considered as string data. Also a string data is used for distinct count measures and keys. SQL Server's default behavior is to store the string data in a file (`.string`) that has a 4GB size limit. This still exists as the default in SQL Server 2012, but this edition introduces a new storage feature called scalable string storage that allows you to overcome this limit. This allows the string store to grow as the data stored increases in size.

Using scalable string storage

This new storage feature increases your upper storage limit to either four billion unique strings or four billion records, whichever is met first, as scalable string storage creates records of a size equal to a 64 KB page. Any strings that are longer than 64KB will not fit into a single record, thereby reducing your limit.

If you have a SQL Server 2012 version of Analysis Services and your dimensions and partitions use the MOLAP (multidimensional) storage engine, you can take advantage of the scalable string feature. You will need to change the value of the `StringStoresCompatibilityLevel` property on your dimension or partition. The default setting with the scalable string storage limit of 4 GB has the value **1050**. To change this to the scalable string storage architecture, you will need to alter this value to **1100**.

The database `CompatibilityLevel` property will also need to be set to **1100**. This is already the default if you used **SQL Server Data Tools** (SSDT) and SSAS 2012 to create or deploy the database. If you have moved a database from a SQL Server 2005 or 2008 to 2012, then you will need to change the compatibility level from 1050 to 1100.

Once you change the `CompatibilityLevel` property to **1100**, you will not be able to attach or restore it on an earlier version of SQL Server.

You will need to use SSAS 2012 to change the `CompatibilityLevel` property to `1100`. If it is an OLAP database (using MOLAP, ROLAP, and HOLAP storage), then you can proceed. Please be aware that if you have a PowerPivot or an SSAS database using xVelocity compression, `CompatibilityLevel` is not supported. Perform the following steps to change the property in a database that was created in a version of SQL Server prior to 2012:

1. Restore or attach your database to your SQL Server 2012 Analysis Services server using **SQL Server Management Studio**.

2. Once you are done, we would recommend you backup the database. Once you have changed the property from **1050** to **1100**, you will not be able to change it back, so it is always a good idea to have a backup of the original.

3. Still in SSMS, connect to your SSAS server that is hosting the database.

4. Right-click on the database name to display the menu and navigate to **Script Database as**, then **ALTER to**, and then select **New Query Edition Window**. This will open an XML representation of the database in a new query window.

5. Using *Ctrl + F*, search for the `CompatibilityLevel` property, which is towards the end of the file.

6. Now change the property from **1050** to **1100**.

7. **Save** the file.

8. To implement the change, click on the **Execute** button located on the query menu.

Now that your databases are configured correctly, we will look at changing the `StringStoresCompatibilityLevel` property. The following steps apply to databases from previous versions of SQL Server, as well as 2012 databases:

1. Open the project containing the dimensions or partitions you want to modify using **SQL Server Data Tools**.

2. If you are altering a *dimension*, open **Solution Explorer** and double-click on the dimension you want to change to bring up **Dimension Designer**.

3. In the **Attributes** pane, select the parent node of the dimension (not a child attribute).

4. Inside the **Properties** pane, go to the **Advanced** section and set the `StringStoresCompatibilityLevel` property to **1100**.

5. Repeat steps 3 and 4 for any other dimensions you want to change.

6. To change a *partition*, open your cube using **Solution Explorer**.

7. Click on the **Partitions** tab and expand the partition.

8. Select the partition you want to change and alter the `StringStoresCompatibilityLevel` to **1100**.

9. Now, **Save** the file.

 Only use the new scalable string storage architecture if you are close to, or have reached the 4GB limit as there is a noticeable performance hit when using it. The increased flexibility you gain will be at the expense of disk space, increased I/O and slower query times.

Summary

In this chapter, you have learned about the new tabular model and which of the three Analysis Services architectures is the best fit for your environment. You saw how to install the three models, determine which model is currently running on your server and how to bypass the default string store limit.

You will probably agree that there is so much to explore in SQL Server 2012 Analysis Services that it deserves a book to itself. If you have not already delved in deep, we hope you have learned enough to start your journey into the world of BI. You are now in a firm position to start exploring the topics we have not had the scope to cover here. One thing is for sure, it is incredibly exciting to see Analysis Services evolve.

In the next chapter, we will explore the new features in Reporting Services, including deprecated features, Data Alerts and Report Builder 2012.

5
Reporting Services

In SQL Server 2008 R2, Microsoft invested heavily in Reporting Services. Compared to previous versions, reports were easier for end users to produce and richer to look at. Shared datasets were introduced, as was the report part gallery, both of which reduced the effort required to create a report through re-use of existing objects. In addition, maps, gauges, spark-lines, data bars and KPIs were introduced to make Reporting Services a much more competitive and visually attractive reporting tool.

In this chapter, we will start by looking at the features that have been deprecated and then explore the landscape that includes Power View and SharePoint. You will find about the exciting new Data Alerts and how your users will benefit. Finally, there is good news for those of you who render reports into Excel or Word format, as there has been improvement here too. So without further ado, let's get started.

Deprecated features

A few things have disappeared in Reporting Services 2012. In particular, if you are still using Semantic Model Definition Language (SMDL) report models, Microsoft's advice is to update your reports to remove the dependency on them. In line with this, the Report Model Designer is not supported by SQL Server Data Tools (SSDT), nor can existing report model projects be opened using SSDT—so you will have to update your reports using the tools from SQL Server 2008 R2 or earlier.

Another change that might catch you out may happen when installing SQL Server from the command line using `setup.exe`. If you want to install SSRS in either the default `NativeMode`, or `FilesOnly` mode, use the `/RSINSTALLMODE` flag on the command line. Conversely, if you wish to switch to a SharePoint installation, use the new flag `/RSSHPINSTALLMODE` to specify a SharePoint installation.

Another feature that has been deprecated from Reporting Services 2012 is Custom Report Items (CRI). We can see the logic behind this: SQL Server 2008 R2 introduced such a diverse range of rich graphical controls into the SSRS toolset, that it is unlikely that most users would have a use for a custom written control— in our experience not many users implemented them.

Finally, BIFF rendering for Word and Excel 1997-2003 files has been removed and is now replaced with the more up-to-date Open XML format which, among other things, permits the rendering of more Excel rows and colors in a report.

Power View and SharePoint modes

Power View, previously known by the codename *Project Crescent*, is a powerful reporting tool, capable of some impressive data visualizations.

As it is only available as a Reporting Services plug-in for SharePoint Server 2010 Enterprise Edition, we have provided the following guidance. This clears up what was a point of great confusion for us prior to writing, and takes you through the three report authoring tools at your disposal when deploying SSRS. Hopefully, this will clarify your thinking as much as it did ours, when it comes to selecting the right tool for the job:

- Power View integrates with SharePoint Server 2010 Enterprise Edition. It is a thin client Silverlight plug-in, aimed squarely at non-technical end-users. It permits professional-looking ad-hoc reports, and powerful data visualizations to be easily created from either PowerPivot workbooks or Analysis Services Tabular models, with a degree of control from the report designer.

A short but useful Power View report tutorial is provided by Microsoft at: `http://technet.microsoft.com/library/hh759325%28v=sql.110%29.aspx`.

A longer set of tutorials on SSRS and Power View 2012 can be found at: `http://www.microsoftvirtualacademy.com/tracks/breakthrough-insights-using-microsoft-sql-server-2012-reporting-services`.

Microsoft has provided some live demonstrations of Power View at the following web page:

`blogs.msdn.com/b/oneclickbi/archive/2011/12/27/more-demos-of-power-view-available.aspx`.

- Report Builder and Report Designer both provide environments for creating .rdl files. Neither requires SharePoint to work.

- Both Report Builder and Report Designer create report definition language (RDL) files.

- Report Builder is a standalone environment for users to create their own reports. Similar conceptually to Power View in that it is a tool aimed squarely at non-technical users, but does not require SharePoint.

- Report Designer is fired up when you open a new SQL Server Data Tools project.

- RDL files are XML files, which store data source, report layout and report data, but not user data. The user data is fetched from a data source, which can be relational or multidimensional.

Note that neither Report Builder nor Report Designer creates data visualizations that are as rich as those offered by Power View. They are more typical of the non-interactive reports that we have grown accustomed to seeing in SSRS.

RDL files created by Report Builder and Report Designer are *not* compatible with Power View. Likewise, Power View creates reports with an RDLX extension, which are not compatible with, or readable by, Report Builder or Report Designer.

Minority Reporting Services

Microsoft is quietly and hastily integrating consumer games technology with business technology. One area where this is already evident is in the unlikely crossover between the Kinect games console and its reporting tools. This uses motion detection to work out a user's movements, eliminating the need for laser pointers or mice, effectively turning any wall into a large touch screen, ideal for presentations.

If you would like to see where Power View is headed, take a look at this short video at:
http://blogs.msdn.com/b/sqlrsteamblog/
archive/2012/01/09/natural-interaction-and-microsoft-
bi.aspx.

Data Alerts

One powerful feature of Power View that is worth being aware of is the **Data Alert**. This allows reports to be sent out when underlying data that is used by a report changes.

This could be a stock value, sales figure, or a new employee. If data is changed, it can trigger a Data Alert, which can send out an email report to one or more recipients. One cool feature is that the alert can be sent out either immediately once the value that is being reported on changes, or at a scheduled time, for example, 04:00, regardless of when the underlying data change took place.

The **Data Alert Designer** allows users to set up and edit Data Alert definitions, while the complementary tool, the **Data Alert Manager** allows Data Alerts to be viewed and edited. Personally, we would like to see them rolled into a single tool. If you do happen to need this feature, it is only available in SharePoint at present, but having the same functionality available in Native Mode SSRS without the need for SharePoint would be a great advantage and selling point. Microsoft, we hope you are listening!

Report Builder 2012

This handy tool is aimed at IT pros and power users and, as a DBA, it is helpful if you need to produce a quick report without becoming involved with Visual Studio. Report Builder is a standalone application that you install on your client machine. It has three wizards to help you create a report quickly and without fuss: Table or Matrix Wizard, Chart Wizard, and Map Wizard. Wizards are great tools for generating a report in super-fast time, but you can also use Report Builder with a blank report and create shared datasets.

 Use Report Builder (current version is 3.0) when you need a report quickly without having to be too involved in Visual Studio development. Using Visual Studio (or SSDT) requires a greater depth of knowledge. It is worth installing a local copy as, if you have reporting as a major focus in your environment, it is bound to come in handy. Download your free copy from: www.microsoft.com/download/en/details.aspx?id=29072.

Excel Renderer for Excel 2007-2010

SSRS reports are typically viewed using ReportViewer from a web page or Windows application, or by running the report from inside Report Builder. Both methods offer the user the ability to manually export the records and format the report into Microsoft Excel. New to SQL Server 2012 is the Excel rendering extension that is compatible with Excel 2007 and 2010. The format is Office Open XML, rendering to an Excel sheet with an .xlsx extension.

The previous limitation of being able to export only 65,000 rows has now been increased to 1,048,576 rows, which is a vast improvement and will be a welcome feature to many end users.

 The Excel 2003 extension is now deprecated but you can still make use of it by following the instructions here, as you need to use the Microsoft Office Compatibility Pack: http://technet.microsoft.com/en-us/library/dd255234(v=sql.110).aspx.

To render a report to Excel 2007 or higher, you continue to do this from the button on the report itself:

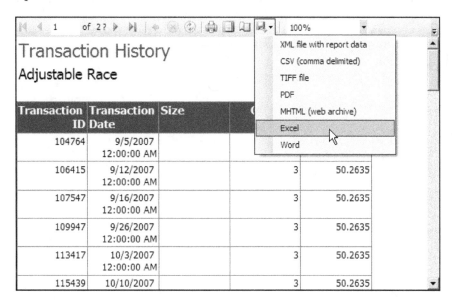

Along with the increased number of rows, the maximum number of columns has now been increased to 16,384 and you can choose from 16 million colors. Add on the capability to ZIP to a compressed file size and it is one rather cool feature. We believe this is one of the best additions to Reporting Services 2012.

Word Renderer for Word 2007-2010

As you may have guessed, along with support for Excel 2007 and 2010 there is also support for Word 2007 and 2010. Again this makes use of the Office Open XML format, rendering to a .docx file. Files rendered to this format will be smaller than previous versions. You can see from the previous screenshot that you can render to Word 2007 or 2010 using the same menu as was used for Excel rendering.

Summary

In this short chapter, we looked at what has been taken out of SQL Server 2012 Reporting Services. Then we learned to distinguish between the different types of reporting tools available to us, followed by a brief introduction to the possibilities of Data Alerts. Finally, we looked at the standalone Report Builder application and took a flying visit to the new rendering abilities for Word and Excel reports.

In the next chapter, we will take a look at some of the major new features in SQL Server Integration Services.

6
Integration Services

SQL Server Integration Services (SSIS) has come a long way. In the early days of SQL Server, the only data transfer facilities available were BCP and SQL Server Transfer Manager. The former is a useful command-line utility still with us today, while the latter was superseded in SQL Server 7.0 by Data Transformation Services (DTS).

While DTS was a definite improvement, it had shortcomings that were difficult to work around. Complex DTS packages were difficult to work with, control flow was tied together with data flow and redeployment was a difficult experience.

In SQL Server 2005, Microsoft released the first version of the Integration Services we know and love today. Seven years on, with SQL Server 2012, SSIS has taken yet another jump forward and is arguably the best Extract, Transform and Load (ETL) tool available from a database vendor.

The SQL Server Data Tools (SSDT) interface has some shiny new enhancements, which are noticeable when developing packages, mostly new icons and buttons that provide shortcuts to sections, such as the variables and parameters windows.

However, the main changes come in the functionality that we are about to see in this chapter. Among other things, we will look at new SSIS functions, demonstrate how shared connection managers allow your packages to use the same connection within a project, the dedicated security role for administering SSISDB and why the new project deployment model brings many benefits.

SSISDB – the SSIS Catalog database

There is a new system database in town! The **SSISDB** catalog holds all of the essential server metadata for SSIS projects that have been deployed to the SSIS server. This includes the package operational history, parameters, environments and the deployment history. The SSISDB database resides on the relational database engine and can be treated like any other database in terms of backup and maintenance, including full, differential and transaction log backups. It stores both the SSIS project and the project deployment .ispac file—an XML format file, which represents the metadata describing the SSIS project. More information can be found at http://msdn.microsoft.com/en-us/library/ff952821(v=sql.105).aspx.

> If you wish to backup and restore SSISDB to another server, you need to follow a few steps in addition to the obvious ones. This article available on the MSDN site details how to deal with backing up and restoring the master key to allow you to restore SSISDB on another server
>
> http://msdn.microsoft.com/en-us/library/hh213291.aspx

Note that although the SSISDB database appears under the database node in Object Explorer, unless you want to directly query the tables and views it contains, most administrative work is performed under the **Integration Services Catalog** node.

For instance, if you wish to change the retention period for a package's operational history, right-click on the catalog's name and select **Properties** from the pop-up menu. The settings can then be changed using the dialog box, as shown in the following screenshot:

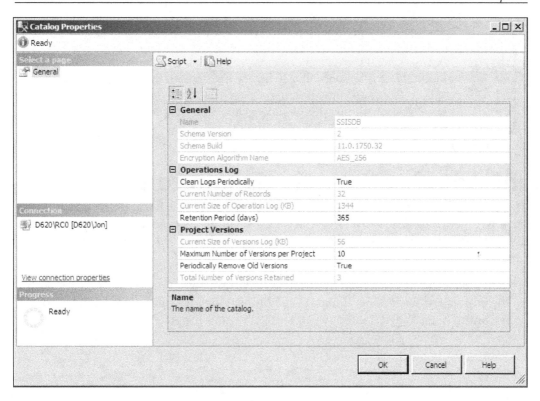

In a busy ETL environment, such as a data warehouse system, it may prove prudent to reduce the **Retention Period** setting to a value less than one year. This is especially true for development and test servers where the ETL process may be run dozens or hundreds of times every day.

Note that if you attempt to run an SSIS 2012 package from SQL Server Management Studio, either directly or from a scheduled job, you may see the following error:

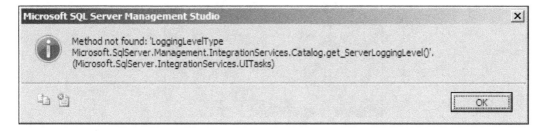

The get_ServerLoggingLevel error message is a documented fault, and is usually caused by upgrading one of the pre-release versions of SQL Server 2012 to RC0 or one of the retail versions. The best way to fix this problem is to uninstall SQL Server and reinstall the retail version.

However, if you really need to run a job from SSMS, you can set up a scheduled job to run an SSIS package manually, ignore the error when it occurs, then just right-click and run the job.

Introducing the ssis_admin role

If you have followed the instructions for creating your SSISDB catalog, you will now be able to add users to a new role for performing administration tasks on the Integration Services server. The new ssis_admin role is a little like the sysadmin role, but just for the SSISDB catalog database.

To add a user to this role, open **Management Studio** and expand the **Security** node in the **Object Explorer** pane. Expand the Logins node and right-click on the account you want to alter. When the menu pops up, click on **Properties**:

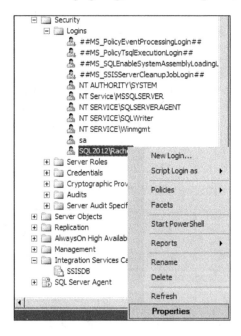

You will first need to ensure that the user is mapped to the SSIS database, so click on the **User Mappings** link on the left-hand side to show the existing databases on the server. Put a check in the box to map the user and set the schema to **dbo**.

[108]

You will notice in the pane in the following screenshot that the list of database roles now contains an additional role called **ssis_admin**. Put a check in this box to add the user to the role and click on the **OK** button to save these settings.

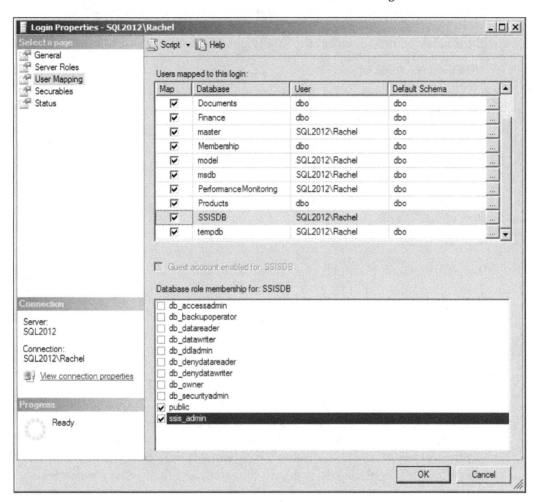

Giving users access to integration services

You are probably thinking that is all very well, but in the Object Explorer window, all I see under the **Integration Services Catalog** node is just the database icon and nothing else. Surely there is more to it than that? And you are right...

If you have worked with SSIS before, you are probably aware that the previous versions allowed all users in the users group to have access to the Integration Services service. Thankfully it is a lot more secure now, but this means you must give users access manually. It is easy enough to do with a handy tool called Component Services. Let us take a look at how to give a user access. In this case, you will probably want to perform the following steps for your account first.

1. Click on the **Start Menu**.

2. Type dcomcnfg.exe in the **Run** textbox to bring up the **Component Services** application window:

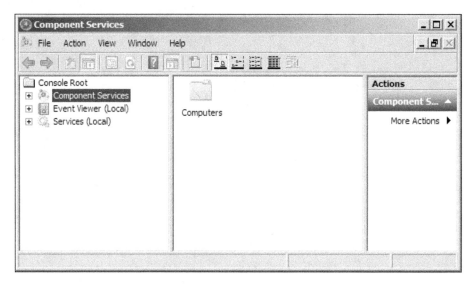

3. Expand the **Component Services** node under the **Console Root**, open **Computers**, then **My Computer** and expand the **DCOM Config** folder. In the right-hand pane, scroll down to **Microsoft SQL Server Integration Services 11.0**, right-click to bring up the menu and then select **Properties**:

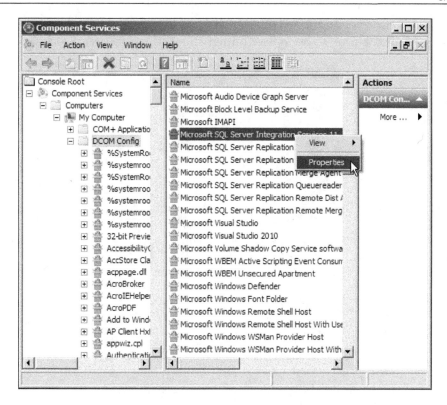

4. This opens the **Microsoft SQL Server Integration Services 11.0 Properties** window:

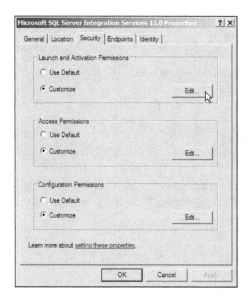

5. Navigate to the **Security** tab as mentioned in the previous step and click on the **Edit...** button to open the **Launch and Activation Permissions** window:

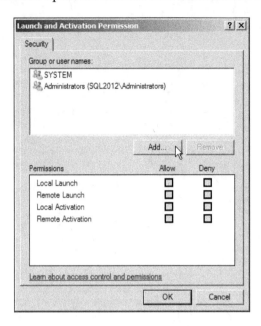

6. Click on the **Add...** button to open the next window:

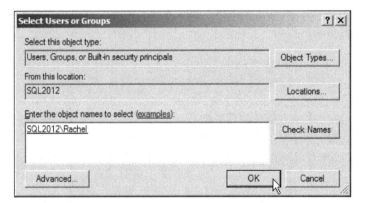

7. Add in the login you want to include and click on **OK**. When you return to the previous screen you will see the user added to the list.

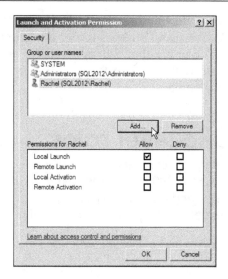

You can continue to add more users in the same way, or if you added your own login, you can now return to **SQL Server Management Studio** and see the database properties in full.

If SSMS was open before adding your login, close and re-open the application, otherwise open **SQL Server Management Studio**. In the **Object Explorer** pane, you will now see that the **SSISDB** database has been added to the **Databases** node:

You can expand the nodes to view and manage all the objects and security. Now, you will notice that the database still appears under the **Integration Services Catalogs** node so, should you or another user be moved from the group you have just been added to, you will still have access to the properties that are available from the right-click menu.

Fixed database-level roles

There are three fixed database-level roles for Integration Services 2012 that are very similar to those available in SSIS 2005 and 2008. You may be wondering why you didn't spot them when we added our user to the ssis_admin role, but that is because they only exist in the msdb database rather than the SSISDB database we created.

These roles, db_ssisadmin, db_ssisltduser and db_ssisoperator allow you to manage user access to your SSIS packages. To add a user to these roles from SSMS:

1. Expand the **Security** node in **Object Explorer**.

2. Expand the **Logins** node.

3. Double-click on the login you want to edit, which brings up the **Login Properties** window:

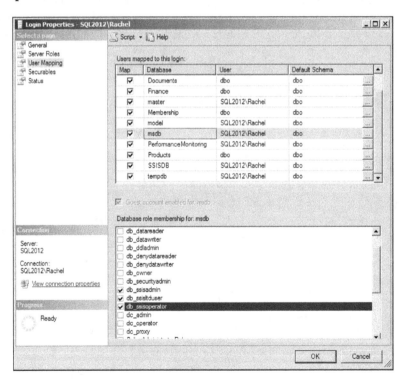

4. Make sure the login has access to the **msdb** database and then select the three roles in the bottom pane. Click on **OK** to save.

You can adjust the permissions of each of these roles to create custom security settings for your environment. Let us take a quick look at how we can prevent users in the **db_ssisadmin** role from deleting packages from our server.

5. Open SSMS and from the **Object Explorer** pane expand the **System Databases** folder and navigate to the **msdb** database. Under **Security | Roles**, open the **Database Roles** node and double-click on the **db_ssisadmin** role or right-click to open the menu and select **Properties**:

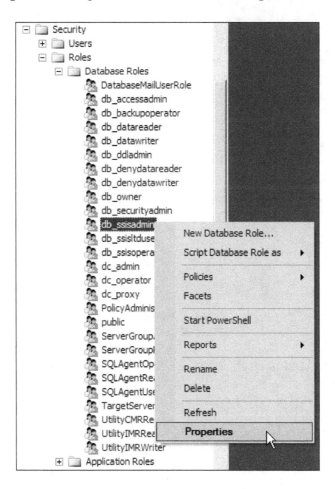

6. This brings up the following window and, as you can see, we only have two users currently in this database role:

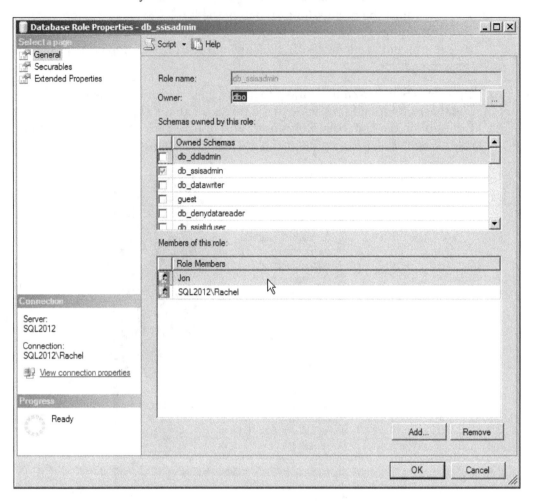

7. In the left-hand pane click on the **Securables** link to view the following:

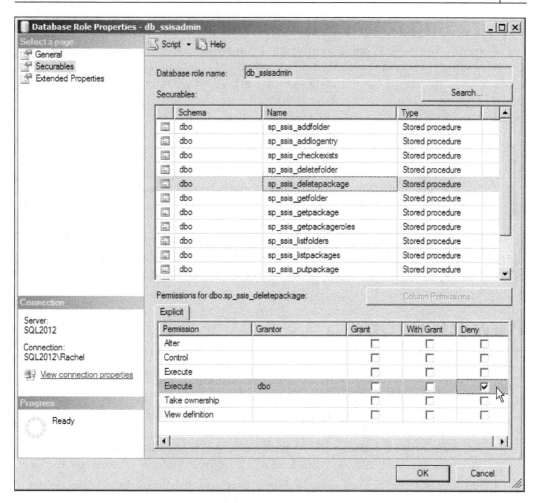

8. Click on the **sp_ssis_deletepackage** in the **Name** column and then in the tab below select the **Deny** checkbox. Click **OK** to save. We have now stopped any logins belonging to this role from deleting packages. You can configure these to your own requirements.

Upgrading from SQL Server 2005 and 2008

If you use the **Upgrade Wizard** to upgrade from either SQL Server 2005 or 2008, then the roles which existed previously will automatically be mapped to the 2012 database roles. In the case of SQL Server 2005 the roles are db_dtsadmin, db_dtsltduser and db_dtsoperator, while in SQL Server 2008 the roles are already named the same as SQL Server 2012.

> We recommend you run the Upgrade Advisor prior to upgrading a previous version to Integration Services 2012. This will highlight any issues that might arise as a result of upgrading your packages to the new 2012 version.

If you are upgrading from a previous version of SQL Server, it is worth taking a look at the **Securables** tab for 2012 (as shown above), as there are fewer **Names** and some of the **Names** have changed to be in line with the current naming conventions.

New functions

SSIS 2012 has introduced four new functions that can be used to manipulate data in components such as the Derived Column Transformation component. The new functions are:

- Left: As its name implies, this takes the left-hand side of a string from a data source. It is useful for operations such as trimming strings, where the target column is not as wide as the source and truncation is deemed to be acceptable; one example would be when mapping Male/Female to M/F.

- ReplaceNull: This is a very powerful feature that allows you to specify on a column by column basis, how nulls will be transformed from a data source. This is particularly useful in data cleansing operations to make null values from source systems consistent and can be used instead of IsNull.

- TokenCount: This is used to return the number of substrings within a string based on a particular token.

- Token: This works with string data types to split up a string based on a particular token. This can be quite useful for parsing addresses from source systems

> A comprehensive list of SSIS 2012 expressions can be found at:
> http://msdn.microsoft.com/en-us/library/ms141671.

Shared connection managers

If you have experience of developing SSIS packages, this is one new feature we think you are really going to like. When creating a package, Integration Services has a wide number of **connection managers** available to enable you to connect to data sources from SQL Server and Analysis Services, to Excel and CSV, as well as FTP, HTTP and more.

A new feature in Integration Services 2012 is the ability to share a connection across multiple packages within your project. Let us take a look at how this works. Open **SQL Server Data Tools (SSDT)** and create a new SSIS project. This will automatically add a new package:

1. In the **Solution Explorer** pane right-click on the **Connection Managers** folder.

2. Choose on **New Connection Manager.**This opens up the **Add SSIS Connection Manager** window:

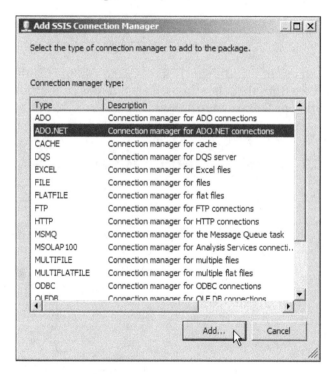

3. Let us choose an **ADO.NET** connection and connect to our local SQL Server. Click on the **Add...** to open the **Configure ADO.NET Manager** window. Click the **New...** button to choose the server and database, then configure the connection:

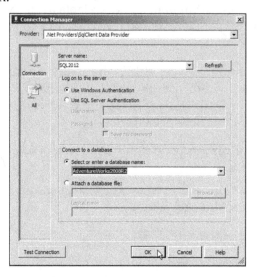

4. Test your connection and then click on **OK** to add the **Connection Manager**. As we can see from the following screenshot, this connection has been added to the existing package in our project:

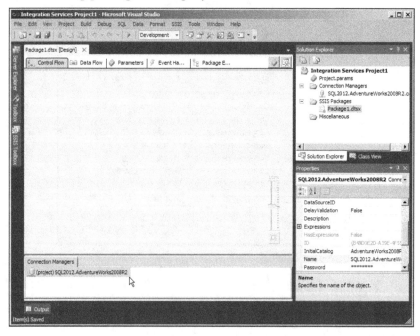

5. Right click on the **SSIS Packages** folder in the **Solution Explorer** pane and choose **New SSIS Package**:

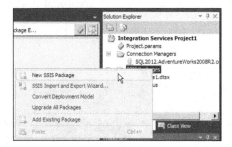

- Add a package to the project and you will see in the **Connection Managers** tab that the connection that we just created has been automatically shared with this package.

Adding a connection manager at the package level

You can of course add a connection to a package that is not shared with every new package you create. Open the package you want to add the connection to and right-click on the **Connection Managers** in the **Solution Explorer** panel. Select **New Connection...** or one of the other connection types from the menu :

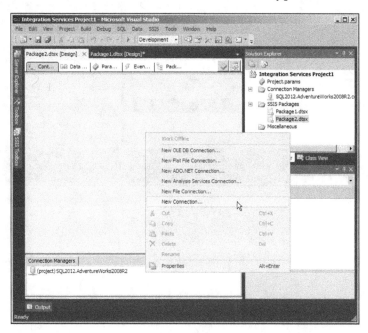

We are going to connect to an Excel spreadsheet, so we will choose to add a new connection. This opens the same **Add SSIS Connection Manager** pane we saw previously. We will browse to an Excel file on the local machine and add this in.

Returning to our package we can now see that the **Excel Connection Manager** has been added to `Package1.dtsx`:

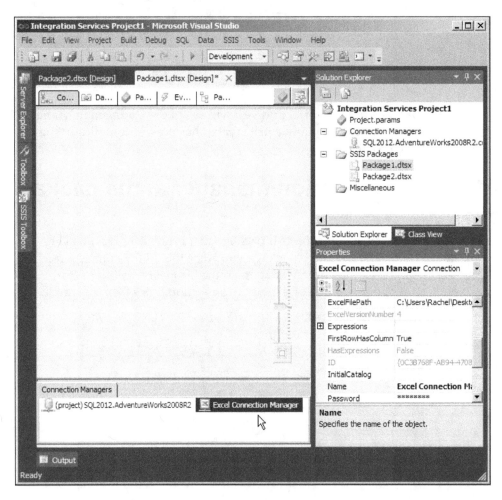

However, when we return to view **Package2.dtsx**, we can confirm that this connection manager does not exist, as we expected:

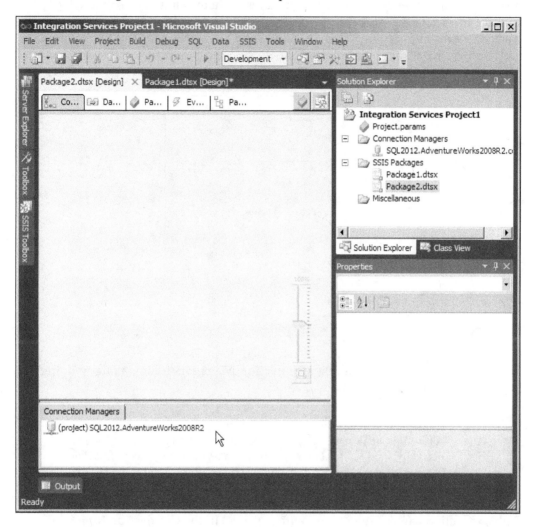

Changing the scope of a connection manager

It is very easy to change a connection manager from existing at project level to package level, or vice versa. To change the **Excel Connection Manager** we just created to exist at the project level, and instantly make this available to Package2 and any future packages we create, right-click on the connection in the **Connection Managers** tab and select **Convert to Project Connection**:

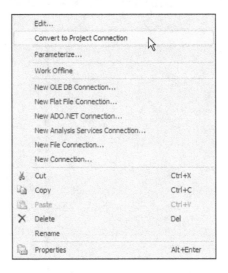

This moves the connection into the **Connection Managers** folder, along with the SQL Server connection we initially created.

Conversely when converting a project connection to a package connection, make sure you are in the context of package the connection needs to be added to. This saves time if you have a number of packages in your project as SSIS will make the connection only available to the current package.

Both connection names are prefixed with (**project**) in the **Connection Managers** tab to help you see the scope of each connection. Follow the same steps to convert a project connection to a package connection.

If you have lots of connections and find opening packages to be slow while Integration Services checks all your connections, you will be pleased to hear that you can now stop this from happening. In the **Connection Managers** tab, right-click a connection and select **Work Offline**. An icon will appear next to the connection to remind you that it is offline. Simply right-click and deselect to go back online.

However, there are two important points to note.

- First, when you put the connection back online (for instance, when you close then re-open a package), it will re-validated, which can take a noticeable amount of time.

- Second, shared connection managers are not unique to a single package. As their name implies, they are shared by *all* of the packages in a project. Unfortunately, this means they get validated with every package too, which can be time consuming.

Enhancements to the Flat File Connection Manager

You can extract and load data from a flat text file using Integration Services. In this version of Integration Services the **Flat File Connection Manager** now supports the ability to parse files with embedded qualifiers. If you have upgraded a SQL Server 2000 DTS package to a newer version of Integration Services and used flat files, you may understand what a benefit this new feature is, as it has caused a lot of development headaches in the past.

Embedded qualifiers surround text fields, as you can see from the following sample row mixing text and data:

```
'Michael', 'Rourke', 37, 'Bristol', 104
```

However, we may have a row containing a name that includes an apostrophe, such as:

```
'Michael', 'O'Rourke', 37, 'Bristol', 104
```

In this case the apostrophe is usually doubled up as follows:

```
'Michael', 'O''Rourke', 37, 'Bristol', 104
```

Previously, SSIS could not handle this scenario and the file would fail to parse. In SSIS 2012, this problem has been fixed and you can now import and parse data that has qualifiers around your text columns, without having to do any additional development to work around it.

Furthermore, the SSIS 2012 Flat File Connection Manager now supports importing variable column, or "ragged right" text files, where data is simply omitted from a column in a text file if it is null. This was a rather annoying and tedious task to support using previous versions of SSIS.

Undo and redo

Microsoft has a history for leading the way in setting standards across all their software offerings, creating consistency with file menus, buttons, short-cut keys and actions. For some reason, every other Microsoft product which allows you to create a document, spreadsheet, e-mail, report and so on, offers you the ability to undo and redo. Integration Services has long been an exception to this rule. Why? We have no idea. The good news is that this has finally been added into Integration Services 2012. Yay!

Now you can undo or redo up to 20 actions in the SSIS Designer and it is available in the Control Flow and Data Flow tabs, Parameters and Event Handlers tabs, and the Variables window. At the project level this feature is now available in the Project Parameters window.

You are no doubt used to using *Ctrl + Z* and *Ctrl + Y* to undo and redo respectively in other Microsoft applications. You can use these, or use the menu items, or roll back or forward through selected items using the arrow next to the menu items. If you have used Visual Studio 2010 for other development work, you will find this to be identical.

Deployment models

SQL Server Integration Services 2012 supports two deployment models: **project** and **package**. The well-known package model is now a legacy model and we are not going to cover this here. There are many advantages to using the new project model that you will benefit from, so we will explore these instead.

As you have probably already guessed, when deploying using the project model all packages are deployed together, whereas the package model deploys just a single package. The project deployment deploys to the SSISDB catalog that we created earlier and which sits under the Integration Services Catalogs folder in the Object Explorer pane in Management Studio. Don't let the name of this folder lead you astray—you can only have one SSISDB catalog per server.

Let us look at some of the advantages and disadvantages of using project rather than package deployment:

- The project, containing all the packages and parameters, is built to a single `.ispac` file. Again this is easier to manage than the package model, which deploys package (`.dtsx`) and configuration (`.dtsconfig`) files to the file system.

- When packages are executed, corresponding events are fired. These events are automatically caught and saved to the SSIS catalog. The advantage of this is that you can query these events using T-SQL views to see what was processed. This is ideal for debugging and tuning your packages.

- Both projects and packages in the SSIS catalog can be validated on the server prior to execution. How do you do this? You can use Management Studio, stored procedures, or managed code, whichever suits you best.

- Parameters are used to assign values to package properties rather than configurations.

- Environment-specific parameter values are stored in environment variables, rather than in configuration files (as is the case with package deployment).

- As the project is deployed in full to Integration Services as a single, atomic unit, it makes it easier to manage and administer. You can query the tables in the SSIS catalog to track packages, projects, folders, environment variables and more.

- However, this brings us to a negative point. As the whole project has to be deployed, it may overwrite perfectly functional packages with one or more packages that do not work.

- Likewise, if your project does not contain a package which is currently present on the server, the package on the server will disappear when the project is deployed.

> Environments are a new feature available to projects that use the project deployment model. An **environment** is a collection of variables that your project can reference. Your project can reference multiple environments, but a single instance of package execution is only able to reference one environment. For example, you can use environments when you have variables that require different values depending on the server environment, such as development, test or production. It is certainly worth exploring, so take a look at the following link to find out more:
>
> http://msdn.microsoft.com/en-us/library/hh213230.aspx

Validating a project or package

We will take a quick look at how easy it is to validate your projects or packages. When you are ready, deploy your projects to Integration Services 2012 from SSDT.

From the file menu select **Project | Deploy**; this brings up a window for you to select the server and the folder to deploy to. Create a new folder if you need to.

Open **Management Studio** and expand the **Integration Services Catalogs** folder in the **Object Explorer**. If you already have Management Studio open, refresh the folder.

You will now see your project folder and all the packages. Right-click on either the project or a package to open up the menu. In our case, we will just validate a single package:

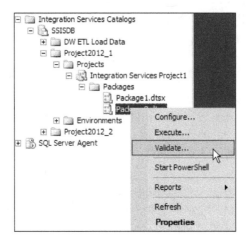

This opens the **Validate Package** window and you can see that the two connections we created previously are available for validation:

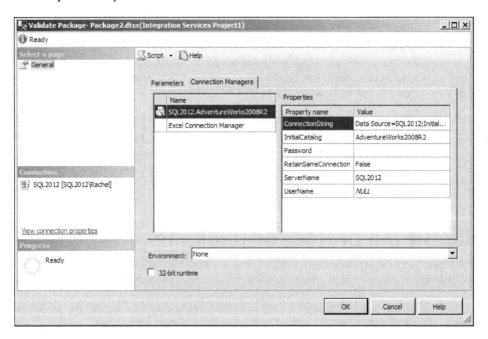

Click on the **OK** button to run the validation. Once finished, you can open the validation report, which lists all the checks that were made to validate the package or project. Our example project is a small package, so this was fairly quick to run. You will need to allow a few minutes for validation on any large scale projects or packages in your environment.

From the menu you have just accessed, you will find the **Reports** menu item, which was available in SSIS 2008. Two standard reports are now available: **All Executions** and **All Validations**. **All Validations** will show you a list of checks, each time you run the validation exercise we just performed. You can create your own reports but it is also worth knowing that you can directly query the SSISDB tables and views to go straight to the data, as we will see in the next section.

Querying the SSISDB

If you don't want to use the reports that are automatically provided by SSIS, you can query the SSISDB directly and return the data you want. You may find the reports are sufficient, but it is worth knowing you can find all the information you need and customize it to your requirements. Let us look at a couple of simple queries.

Open a new query window, connect to the **SSISDB** database and execute the following:

```
SELECT * FROM [catalog].[packages]
```

As you have probably guessed, this returns a list of all the packages deployed to the server:

	package_id	name	package_guid	description	package_format_version
1	1	Package1.dtsx	12BAB322-410C-4E3E-A3D5-8759CBE03B29		6
2	2	Package2.dtsx	4B6B8B08-7776-4316-B83B-BF064B3C7428		6
3	3	Package.dtsx	48D3EFA4-B03B-40D1-B345-59C44FCAE287		6
4	4	Package.dtsx	AC811670-AD81-4B7E-8C9A-0A6C34F92879		6

Scroll to the columns on the right-hand side and you can find out the major, minor and build version numbers, version comments, and the time the package was last validated.

We will take a look at one more example. Clear your query window and execute the following:

```
SELECT * FROM [catalog].[projects]
```

Scroll to the right and you can see who has created which packages, when they were created, and when they were last deployed:

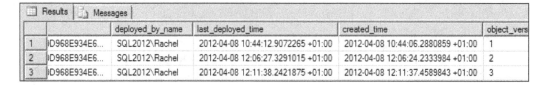

While the standard reports will probably provide you with all that you need, querying the SSISDB directly can sometimes be a faster option and allows you to see data across all projects and packages on the server.

> We recommend that you explore the tables and views in the SSISDB catalog to see what data is available and might be useful to you. There are some interesting data that can help you debug and develop your projects, so spend some time exploring.

Comparing and merging packages

Package formats have been given some consideration in this version of Integration Services, which now makes it easier to compare your packages. This neater XML format also gives you the ability to merge packages that do not have conflicting changes.

By using XML, the format allows for a separate element for each property and the attributes are listed in alphabetical order so it is easy to find and understand the settings. Properties that have a default value won't be listed, while elements that appear more than once are now contained within a parent element.

If you have objects in a package that can be referenced by other objects, which is usually most of them, you will find they have been given a `RefID` attribute. Rather than using a long), `GUID` (globally unique identifier), this `RefID` is unique and can be read and understood. This comes in handy when merging changes between two packages as the RefID can be used to check that all references to an object have been updated correctly.

Color coded and indicator status codes

One small but welcome improvement to SSIS 2012 has been a change in the way that status information about a component is displayed when running a package.

As shown in the following screenshot, the visual indicator is still in color, but also gives a non-color based indicator (a tick or a cross) of the state of the task after running:

This is good news for those of us who are both developers and red-green color blind (around 7 to 10 percent of the male population, < 0.5 percent of the female population). Furthermore, it is useful when printing a black and white screenshot of a running package for documentation purposes.

 If you are not sure if you are color blind, search for an online version of the Ishihara Test.

Package execution logs

Although it has been available since SQL Server 2005, SSIS logging has been fairly basic. Most developers have coded some sort of custom logging to make up for the inadequacies in SSIS. However, in SQL Server 2012, SSIS can automatically provide more detailed runtime logging to a table, text file, the Windows event log, XML file, or even a SQL Server Profiler trace.

Logging can be enabled for all SSIS tasks at the package level, or it can be enabled just for individual tasks at the component level, without enabling it at the parent package level. In addition, logging can be written to multiple logs from the same package or task, which gives great flexibility.

Furthermore, even the events that are logged and the information for each event can be specified. All of this is done via the **Configure SSIS Logs** dialog box in the **SSIS Designer** interface in **SQL Server Data Tools**.

Jamie Thomson has put together an excellent article about the enhanced SQL Server 2012 SSIS logging capabilities at:

```
http://sqlblog.com/blogs/jamie_thomson/
archive/2011/07/16/ssis-logging-in-denali.aspx.
```

How to set up basic SSIS logging

Perform the following steps to set up basic logging:

1. In SSDT, open the SSIS package and click on the **Data Flow** tab.
2. Then click on the SSIS menu, and select the **Logging…** menu item.
3. Select logging at either the **Package** level, or the **Data Flow Task** level.
4. Select the **Provider type** from the drop down – in this case pick a text file.
5. Click on the **Add…** button. Note that this can be done multiple times for each type of log.
6. Against each log type, click on the **Configuration** cell to set up where you would like the logging to take place.
7. Finally, click on the **Details** tab, and select those events you would like to log.

You should now see a dialog box set up like the one in the following screenshot. Click on **OK**, and run your SSIS package:

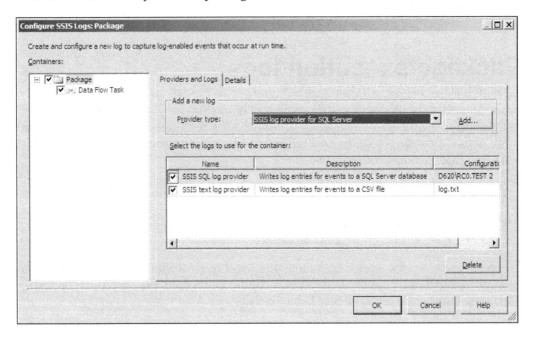

View the results of logging

Be aware that in the previous example, while we specified the filename for the text file, the server and database names, we didn't give the logging dialog box the name of a table where the logging information should be stored.

This is because SSIS creates the table name by default. However, finding it isn't immediately obvious, as it is classified as a system table!

> If you want to find SSIS logging information that has been written to SQL Server, it is in the database you specified in the SSIS logging options, written to a system table called `dbo.sysssislog`.

While the information captured is useful for troubleshooting package execution problems, personally we would like to see Microsoft amend this so that it is not classified as a system table, or at the very least give us an opportunity to specify the name of a logging table of our own choice. On data warehouse systems, this table is quite capable of becoming massive in a single night, so it would be good to have the option to split logging from different processes into separate tables, if we so choose.

Package execution reports

Once the **SSISDB** has been created, package execution reports can be accessed from **SSMS** by right clicking on the **Integration Services Catalog** node:

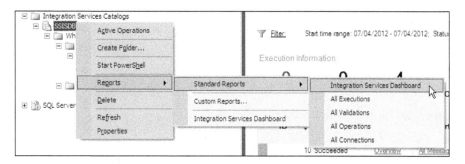

A typical SSIS package report can be seen in the following screenshot and allows detailed drill-through into the performance and error message levels:

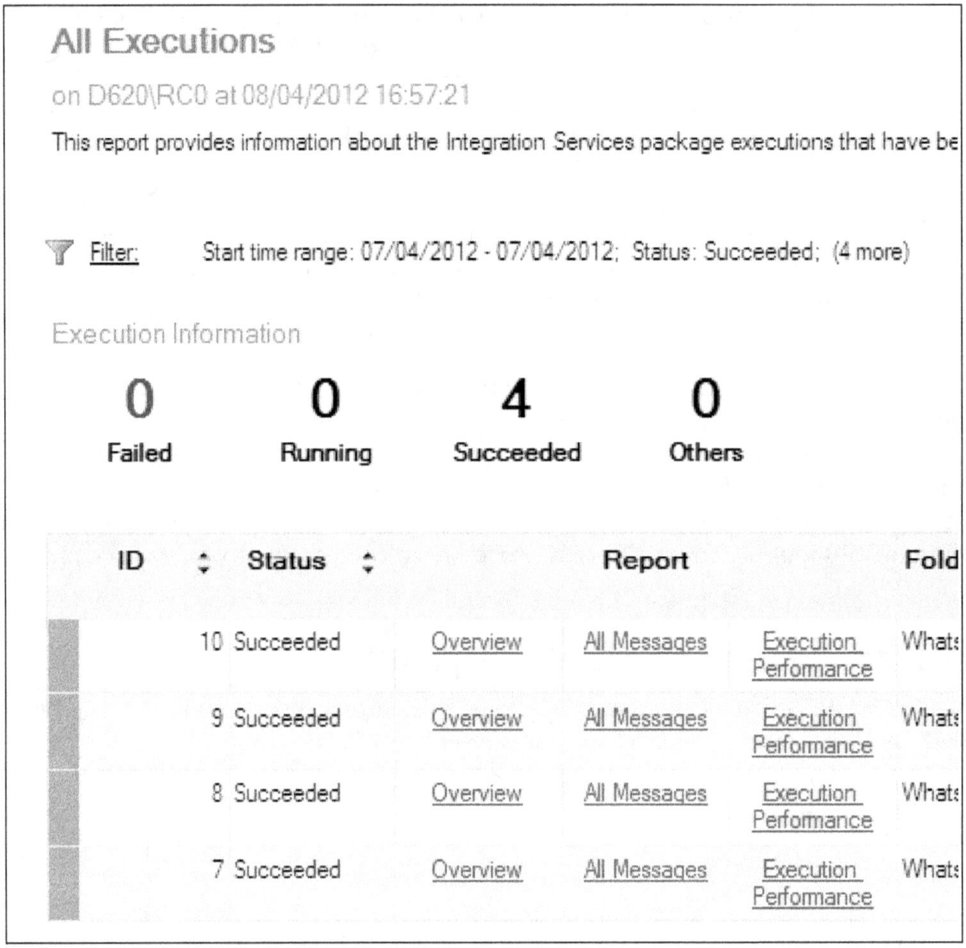

All Executions

on D620\RC0 at 08/04/2012 16:57:21

This report provides information about the Integration Services package executions that have be

▽ Filter: Start time range: 07/04/2012 - 07/04/2012; Status: Succeeded; (4 more)

Execution Information

0	0	4	0
Failed	Running	Succeeded	Others

ID	⇕	Status	⇕	Report			Fold
10		Succeeded		Overview	All Messages	Execution Performance	Whats
9		Succeeded		Overview	All Messages	Execution Performance	Whats
8		Succeeded		Overview	All Messages	Execution Performance	Whats
7		Succeeded		Overview	All Messages	Execution Performance	Whats

One really neat feature is that you can now see at a glance if an ETL job is taking longer than expected with an easy-to-read graph of the last 10 package execution times:

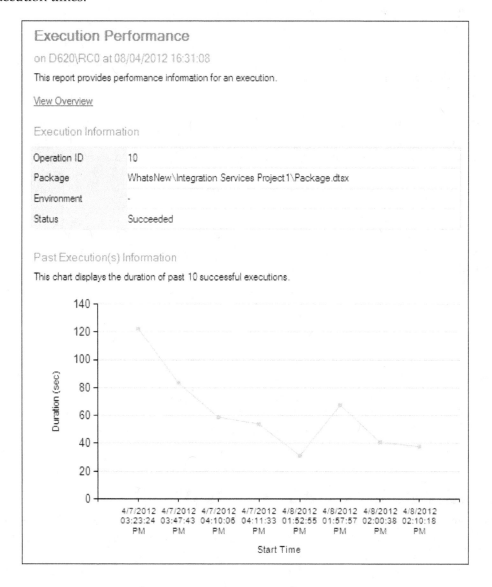

Expression indicators

Expression indicators are a simple but good idea, especially when moving SSIS packages from development and test environments into production. You can already parameterize previously hard-coded values such as connection strings in the connection manager. This allows the server or environment in which the package is running to be detected by the package and the appropriate connection string used, without requiring the manual intervention of the DBA, with all the time and risk that entails.

However, up until SQL Server 2012, SSIS did not give an indication as to whether an expression was used within a connection. Now, you can determine it at a glance. Previously a connection manager that was expressionless would look like this:

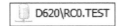

Now, with an expression embedded in it (and that is for any property, not just a connection string), the same Connection Manager will change appearance to look like this:

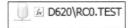

Simple, but effective.

 If you want to explore expressions in your package, take a look at BIDS Helper. This handy addition to Visual Studio and SQL Server Data Tools can be downloaded from: `http://bidshelper.codeplex.com`.

Change Data Capture support

Fundamentally, **Change Data Capture** (CDC) allows you to load just those changes that have been applied to data in a source system since the last time you loaded data from it, without having to make any schema changes to the source system in order to track them. This has obvious uses in the data warehousing world, where requesting a full load of a large source system's data or altering its schema is impractical, and you need just the data since the last time you loaded it.

SSIS 2012 introduces three new components to reduce the complexity of the plumbing required to create a CDC-based data loading system. Those components are:

- **CDC Control Task:** This new component is used to manage the lifetime, or scope, of a change data capture session. It can automatically record first load start and end points for a CDC load and retrieve or record the range of CDC values that are processed. It is found on the task toolbar for the **SSIS Control Flow** tab in **SQL Server Data Tools**.

- **CDC Source:** This component is used to query the tables that store the CDC changes from the source systems and distribute them to other SSIS components. It is located in the **Other Sources** section of the toolbox for the Data Flow designer. The CDC Source component has several modes that allow it to act in different manners according to what is required, such as aggregate ("net") changes, all changes, all changes with before and after values, and so on. The one you choose will be dictated by your business' needs.

Matt Masson has documented the CDC Source control's modes on his blog at:

http://www.mattmasson.com/index.php/2012/01/processing-modes-for-the-cdc-source/.

- **CDC Splitter:** Finally, there is the CDC splitter component, which can be found in the SSDT toolbox under the Other Transforms section for the Data Flow designer.

This component is a conditional splitter, in that it splits data from the CDC source into different data flows for inserts, deletes and updates, so that they can be handled appropriately by the target system. This permits great flexibility for data warehouse usage, which is where these components are most likely to be used.

It is worth reading Matt Masson's excellent article on using CDC at:

`http://www.mattmasson.com/index.php/2011/12/cdc-in-ssis-for-sql-server-2012-2/?utm_source=rss&utm_medium=rss&utm_ campaign=cdc-in-ssis-for-sql-server-2012-2`

There are data warehouse books which cover CDC in detail so we won't get into the details of how to use it here. Suffice to say that if you are loading data from a source system, that is either heavily loaded, created by a third party, or otherwise difficult to alter, and don't want to perform full loads or use replication to attempt to get around the problem, then CDC is the way to go. These new components in SSIS 2012 definitely take the pain out of building a solution to that problem.

Data taps

The last significant new feature of SSIS that we will look at is the **data tap**. A data tap literally "taps into" the data flow between SSIS tasks and writes it out to a `.csv` file.

This is very useful, especially in a production environment, as it allows a dump of the data passing between two SSIS tasks to be captured for analysis by a production, test, or development team if there is a production problem, without changing the SSIS package in the live environment.

This means the production DBA doesn't need to change the package (always a bad idea) and the developer doesn't have to be given access to the production machine in order to get the data they need to debug the process. Everyone wins, including the end users, as the system remains in the same stable state.

A data tap is transient, so each time you execute a package, you need to recreate the data tap, which just involves a call to three T-SQL stored procedures.

As this functionality is most likely to be used in a production environment, this transience is a sensible default. It means that a data tap will not inadvertently be left in place, potentially hitting SSIS package performance, nor will it create data files that grow until they use up all of the available disk space.

Setting up a Data Tap

Creating a data tap is easy. You will need two things before you begin: Access to the server where the SSIS package is deployed, and also to the development box where the package was created (or at least the project that was created and a copy of SQL Server Data Tools). You will need information from both of these places, as we are going to plug it into a couple of stored procedure calls to create the data tap.

For this example we will use a basic SSIS package that just copies data from a SQL Server table to a flat file. We want to put the data tap on the first data flow, between the **OLE DB Source** and the **Copy Column** task:

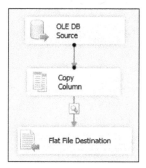

First, open up the deployed package on the SSIS server. Find the folder name, project name, and package name:

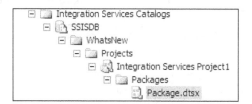

In the previous example, the folder is **WhatsNew**, the project is named **Integration Services Project1**, and the package is **Package.dtsx**. Open up **SQL Server Management Studio**, create a new query and enter the following code, plugging in the values obtained previously:

```
USE [SSISDB]
/* Step 1: Create an execution instance for the package containing the
data flow you want to tap into.
The information for this call comes from SSMS, Integration Services
Catalog, after you have deployed the SSIS package to the target
server.
*/
```

```
DECLARE @return_value int,
        @execution_id bigint
EXEC @return_value = [catalog].[create_execution]
        @folder_name = N'WhatsNew',
        -- Name of the folder in the SSISDB catalog from SSMS
        @project_name = N'Integration Services Project1',
        -- Name of the project in the SSISDB catalog from SSMS
        @package_name = N'Package.dtsx',
        -- Name of the package to execute from SSMS
        @execution_id = @execution_id OUTPUT
```

Great, we are half way there! Now open the original project file (either on your machine or have a word with the developer). You will need two more pieces of information in addition to deciding the filename of the data tap file that will be produced on the SSIS server.

 Note that is is not possible to set the path of the output file. All data taps get written to the same folder, C:\Program Files\Microsoft SQL Server\110\DTS\DataDumps.

Perform the following steps to run a data tap:

1. Look at the SSDT project and click on the **Data Flow Task** tab.

2. Note the value of the **PackagePath** property for the Data Flow Task itself, which should be something like **\Package\Data Flow Task**:

3. Next, click on the **Data Flow** link that you want to tap into—in this case, the one between the OLE DB source and the Copy Column Component. Look at its **Properties** sheet and copy the value of the **IdentificationString** property, in this case **Paths[OLE DB Source.OLE DB Source Output]**:

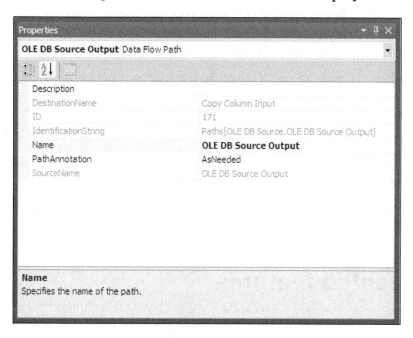

4. Once you have both of those values and have decided on the filename where the tapped data will be written, plug them into the second stored procedure call, as shown in the following block of code:

```
/* Step 2 : Now add a data tap to a data flow - the information
for this call comes from SSDT
*/
DECLARE @data_tap_id bigint
EXEC   @return_value = [catalog].[add_data_tap]
          @execution_id = @execution_id,
-- from the previous call to create_execution stored proc
          @task_package_path = N'\Package\Data Flow Task',
-- To find this value, open the package in SSDT, click on the Data
Flow tab, and look at its Properties - PackagePath is the one you
need
          @dataflow_path_id_string = N'Paths[OLE DB Source.OLE
DB Source Output]', -- click on the data flow (not the task) you
want to tap in SSDT, look at its Properties, and copy the value in
the IdentificationString property
          @data_filename = N'DataTapOutputFile.csv', -- NOTE
```

> This CANNOT be written to a path, only to the default folder,
> "C:\Program Files\Microsoft SQL Server\110\DTS\DataDumps" at the
> time of writing
>
> ```
>            @data_tap_id = @data_tap_id OUTPUT
> ```

5. Now add a third and final call to the code in order to run the package;

```
-- Step 3: Finally, run the package
EXEC   catalog.start_execution @execution_id
```

6. Execute the code and wait while the package is run. Note that if the data tap is re-created without deleting the previous file, a new file will be created with the file name suffix (n).csv to indicate the sequence in which it was created.

Although there is no visual interface, once the package has been executed, the run can be seen in the SSIS package execution report

As previously described the data tap output can be found in C:\Program Files\ Microsoft SQL Server\110\DTS\DataDumps on the SSIS server. The tap can be run multiple times without making any changes and each run will create a new data tap file.

Deprecated features

Histogram, **Scatter Plot** and **Chart Data Viewers** have all been removed as data viewers. However, the grid view still remains, which is appropriate as it is the only one most developers ever used.

Resources

There are a few other minor tweaks to features in SSIS 2012, which we have not had space to explore fully in this chapter, including small changes to the row count transformation and pivot task. If you would like to explore these further, the following resources may prove useful.

- Microsoft's own SSIS team blog can be found at: http://blogs.msdn. com/b/mattm/.

- Another useful SSIS 2012 site run by Phil Brammer can be found at http:// www.ssistalk.com - he is also available on Twitter at @PhilBrammer.

- Finally, Microsoft have a page dedicated to the new features in SSIS at:

  http://msdn.microsoft.com/en-us/library/bb522534(SQL.110).aspx

Summary

In this chapter we looked at the most important new features of SQL Server Integration Services 2012, from the new catalog database and admin roles for DBAs, through to data taps, SSIS reports, package comparison, the addition of the undo feature, and the new deployment modes among others.

In the next chapter we will take a look at a brand new part of SQL Server, which is Data Quality Services. We will show you what it is capable of and take you through a brief tutorial on how to use it.

7
Data Quality Services

Operational data quality is a big issue, everywhere. Numerous surveys identify it as a major challenge and cost that IT departments and business alike must tackle. Data quality reflects on the business when a customer calls. It consumes call center time when customer records are incorrect and have to be corrected. It impacts on the aggregate information we create from our operational data when we build a data warehouse. It directly affects the usefulness of the information we extract from data mining projects. Furthermore, it causes us uncertainty when we read inaccurate reports.

It is this last point that is perhaps the most worrisome. If a report sits in the hands of your CEO, it is because he or she needs that information to make a business decision. At this level, the decision is likely to be a strategic one, guiding the corporation in

one direction or another, possibly part of a long term plan. If the decision is right, everyone concerned will do well. If it is wrong, you or your colleagues could be looking for a new job. The results are disparate and in the case of the latter, all because the data that created the information in the report was incorrect, inaccurate, or incomplete.

SQL Server 2012 introduces a new tool called Data Quality Services (DQS). DQS has one purpose — to cleanse data in the fastest, most efficient and reliable way possible. Not only that, but it lets you re-use the knowledge gained from one data cleansing exercise in another.

This chapter looks at some of the basics of DQS, a tool that is likely to become a major part of the SQL Server toolkit. We are about to dive in with a quick tour and tutorial to provide you with a sample of its capabilities. At the end of this chapter you will be able to install and configure DQS, and apply some basic data cleansing techniques to increase the quality of your data.

Reasons for using Data Quality Services

Data Quality Services is only available in SQL Server Business Intelligence and Enterprise editions. You can choose to install the service during the normal installation of the database engine, or add it later on.

DQS allows domain experts, often referred to as subject matter experts (SMEs) or data stewards, to improve the quality of data. This is good because it lifts the load from developers and DBAs who are rarely experts in the format and valid values of business data. However, that is not to say DBAs and developers can't use it; they can, and to great effect if they know the data, and now DQS can help achieve this.

DQS allows the data steward to create, refine and use reference data, as well as associate reference data with operational input data, whose quality needs to be improved. It produces a set of output data in the form of a new dataset, either in a table or in a CSV file. It does not alter the existing operational data, that is left to the DBA or developer to decide how best to handle, and is not a part of DQS.

So, why would you want to use DQS? Why not just manually cleanse the data, either by directly editing it or updating it with T-SQL? By using DQS, SMEs can easily become involved and leverage their business knowledge to improve the quality of the data during the data cleansing exercise. DQS combines human and machine intelligence and provides the ability to easily and manually review the data cleansing output with very little effort.

Furthermore, DQS uses custom data mining algorithms to perform machine cleansing, based on reference data and rules. The quality of the knowledge base drives the quality of the results, just as in any other data mining exercise. Moreover, DQS can be functionally integrated with SSIS at the programmatic level, which is a very exciting prospect.

You can use Data Quality Services to quality check the following attributes in your data:

Quality	Example
Accuracy	If a customer's loan is paid off, should they still be in the database?
Duplication	Are Dave Smith and David Smith the same customer?
Completeness	Should those NULLs, empty strings and zeros be in the database?
Conformity	M/Male/MALE/1 – Keep the values uniform, even if they mean the same thing. This is a common problem in data warehouses when data is pulled in from multiple legacy systems, each with their own way of representing the same data.
Validation	Do birth dates, salary payments, loan amounts, and mortgage terms fall within an acceptable range?

Installing Data Quality Services

Before you get started, you will need to install DQS. This is done from the SQL Server installation media. If you remember in *Chapter 1, Installing SQL Server 2012*, when we installed SQL Server, the **Data Quality Services** checkbox was listed under the **Database Engine Services** option as shown in the following screenshot:

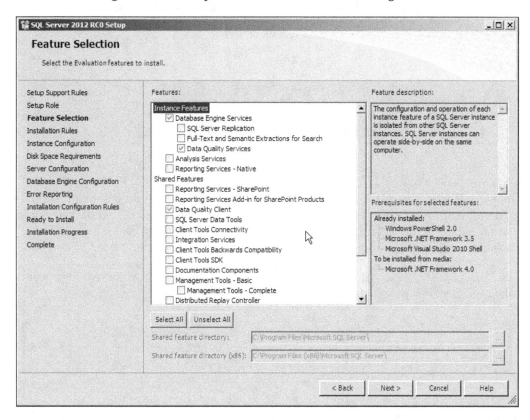

As shown in the previous screenshot, there are two parts to Data Quality Services – the engine and the client. Install the engine on your server and the client on the PC from which you want to access it, in the same way you install the database engine on one server and the management tools on your own PC.

 If you reinstall DQS, remember that any knowledge base you have built will be overwritten, so proceed with caution.

If Data Quality Services is not already installed, use your installation media to run through the setup to add it. If you are not sure if you have installed DQS already, have a look on the program menu under Microsoft SQL Server 2012 to see if it is listed, as shown in the following screenshot:

Once you have installed DQS, open your file menu, as seen previously, and choose **Data Quality Server Installer**. A DOS prompt will appear, and you will be prompted for a password for the **Database Master Key**. This must be *at least* eight characters and a combination of character types to make it strong. If you have previously installed DQS, you will be given the option of whether or not to re-install it.

The Data Quality Server Installer creates the DQS databases, DQS service logins and roles, and a stored procedure in the master database called DQInitDQS_MAIN.

> If anything goes wrong during the installation, check the installer
> log at: C:\Program Files\Microsoft SQL Server\
> MSSQL11.<instance_name>\MSSQL\Log.

Once you have successfully run the installer, there are three more things you need to do.

Enabling TCP/IP for remote access to the DQS server

First, you will need to enable the TCP/IP network protocol so that you can remotely connect to the DQS:

1. From your program menu, open **Microsoft SQL Server 2012**.
2. Click on **Configuration Tools**.
3. Click on **SQL Server Configuration Manager**.

4. Once the configuration window has opened, expand the **SQL Server Network Configuration** node in the left-hand side pane.

5. In the right-hand console pane, click on **Protocols for <instance_name>**.

6. Click on **SQL Server Services**.

7. If **TCP/IP** is not already enabled, right-click and choose **Enable**. If you change this property, you will need to restart the SQL Server service for it to take effect.

Making data accessible for DQS operations

In order for DQS to see the data you want to cleanse, it will need to have access to it. Next, we will walk through the steps required to map the users and roles required to grant this access:

1. From **Management Studio**, expand your instance node and then expand **Security**. Expand **Logins** and choose the DQS login to apply the changes to.

2. Right-click and choose **Properties**.

3. Click on **User Mapping** on the left-hand side of the screen, and under the **Map** column put a check in the checkbox next to **DQS_STAGING_DATA**.

4. In the pane below, put a check next to the following roles – **db_datareader, db_datawriter** and **db_ddladmin**.

Granting a DQS role on DQS_Main for DQS users

Open SQL Server Management Studio and connect to your SQL Server instance using the following steps:

1. Expand the **Security** node in the **Object Explorer** pane, click on Logins, then double-click on the user who needs access to DQS.

2. On the left side, click on the **User Mapping** page.

3. Check the **DQS_Main** checkbox in the top right pane.

4. In the **Database Role Membership** box, grant access to **dqs_administrator, dqs_kb_editor,** and **dqs_kb_operator,** as is applicable to the level of access you wish to apply.

5. Click on the **OK** button to apply these changes.

Now that you have run the installation, we will move on to using DQS.

> Once you have installed DQS, three new databases will appear in SQL Server Management Studio. These are DQS_MAIN, DQS_PROJECTS, and DQS_STAGING_DATA. Don't forget to add them to your backup and maintenance plans.

Using Data Quality Services

Now let us jump straight into using DQS. We will begin by creating a basic table in SQL Server, which has some valid and invalid data that needs cleansing. Here is the table we are going to use for this example, followed by the code that created it:

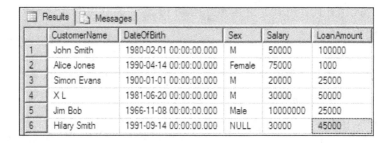

	CustomerName	DateOfBirth	Sex	Salary	LoanAmount
1	John Smith	1980-02-01 00:00:00.000	M	50000	100000
2	Alice Jones	1990-04-14 00:00:00.000	Female	75000	1000
3	Simon Evans	1900-01-01 00:00:00.000	M	20000	25000
4	X L	1981-06-20 00:00:00.000	M	30000	50000
5	Jim Bob	1966-11-08 00:00:00.000	Male	10000000	25000
6	Hilary Smith	1991-09-14 00:00:00.000	NULL	30000	45000

The following code creates the table shown in the previous screenshot:

```
CREATE DATABASE TEST
GO

CREATE TABLE Customer
(
  CustomerName  varchar(200),
  DateOfBirth   datetime,
  Sex           char(10),
  Salary        int,
  LoanAmount    int
)

GO

INSERT INTO Customer
VALUES   ('John Smith', '01/February/1980', 'M', 50000, 100000),
         ('Alice Jones', '14/April/1990', 'Female', 75000, 1000),
         ('Simon Evans', '01/January/1900', 'M', 20000, 25000),
```

```
('X L', '20/June/1981', 'M', 30000, 50000),
('Jim Bob', '08/November/1966', 'Male', 10000000,
        25000),
('Hilary Smith', '14/September/1991', null, 30000,
        45000)


SELECT    *
FROM    Customer
```

Understanding the interface is the key to understanding the DQS workflow. Open up the **Data Quality Client** from the SQL Server folder in the **Programs** menu, and this is the first screen you will see:

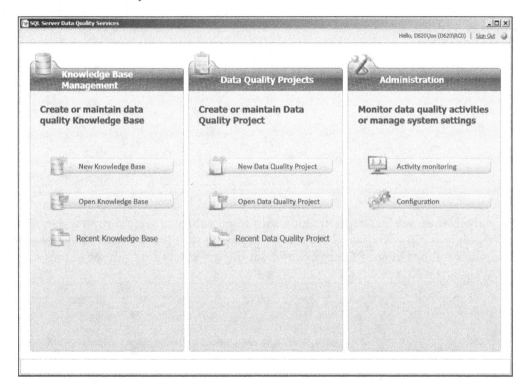

The main page is set out to match the workflow so you complete tasks from left to right. The knowledge base contains the reference data that is used to cleanse the operational data. Once built, the knowledge base has the benefit that it can be re-used to cleanse the data sets of other, similar operational systems. The knowledge base is then maintained with the Knowledge Base Management tool.

The **Data Quality Projects** tab, or tool, is where the data cleansing operation takes place. The Administration tool is used for tool and DQS service administration. Click on the **New Knowledge Base** button and the following screenshot appears:

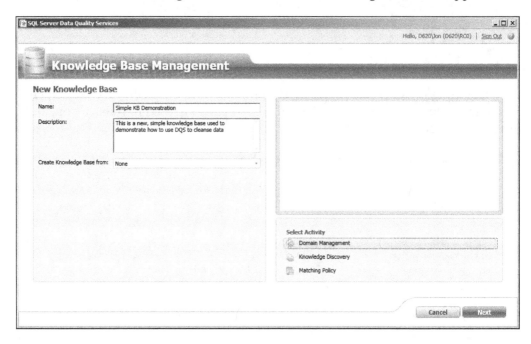

Fill in the **Name** and **Description** fields with some values of your choosing, as shown in the previous screenshot, and then click on **Next** to start the **Domain Management** task. Click on the **Create a Domain** button at the top left, as you can see in the following screenshot:

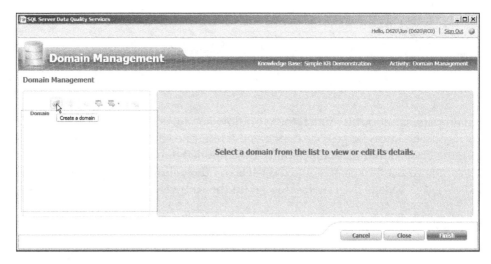

Understanding domains

A **domain** is the set of values that a column in the operational database can contain. In DQS it extends this concept to include the idea of a rule, somewhat analogous

to a SQL Server constraint. Rules are useful as they allow us to create complex conditions that are an easier way to express a set of defined values. A set of values can theoretically be infinite, such as an integer series, so a rule is a more concise way to describe it.

For example, $0 <= Age <= 150$ instead of $\{0,1,2,3,4,5,...,148,149,150\}$.

The first implicitly defines the set using a rule, while the second explicitly defines the set as a list of all the values it can contain. The latter is fine for small domains such as $\{M,F\}$, but not for large sets of values or conditional rules, such as a maximum loan amount, which may need to be calculated based on deposit and salary values.

The following screenshot shows how to create a domain:

Click on the **OK** button. We have now created a domain. But we have not yet defined the list of valid values. This is done as shown in the next screenshot:

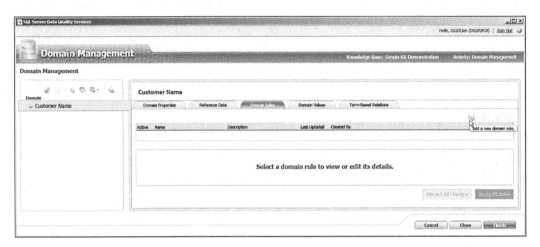

Click on the **Domain Rules** tab, then click on the small green **+** sign to add a new rule. It is here that you define the rules for values which are valid in the Customer domain. Note the word "domain". The domain is not yet linked up to any columns in the operational database, so it is merely a rule in isolation inside the DQS knowledge base, and it is not yet attached to any operational databases, as shown in the following screenshot:

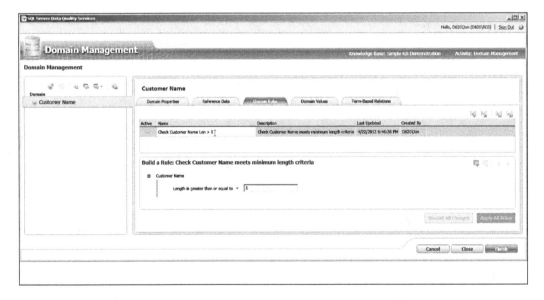

Now let us add another rule, this time to ensure that the Loan Amount does not exceed a maximum value. Click on the **Create a domain** button (top left, beneath **Domain Management**):

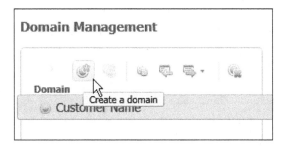

Choose a name for the new domain, add a brief description and select its data type, as shown in the following screenshot:

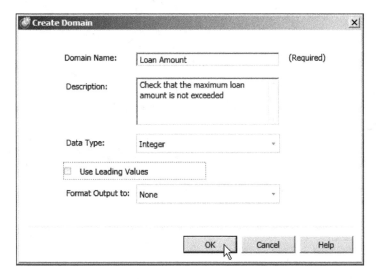

This time we are going to add a rule to ensure that any loan amount is at least **$10,000** in size, as shown in the following screenshot:

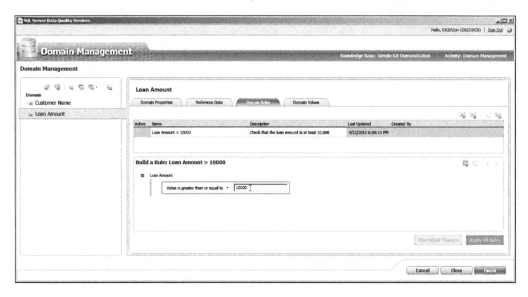

Now click on the **Finish** button in the lower right-hand corner of the screen to complete the rule building process. When asked to confirm, click on the **Publish** button:

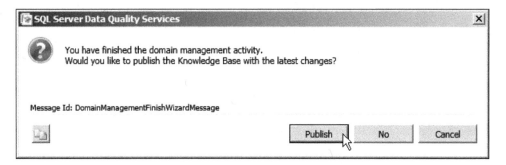

Once this has been successfully published, you will see the following message appear to confirm it:

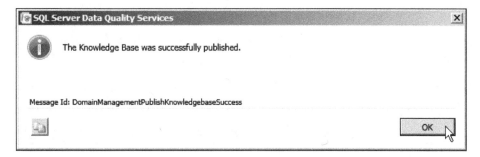

Click on **OK**, and you will be redirected to the main screen.

Microsoft's guide to getting the best performance out of DQS, Data Quality Services Performance Best Practices Guide, can be found at: www.microsoft.com/download/en/details.aspx?id=29075.

Coupling rules to data: the Data Quality Project

We have now created a basic knowledge base. This knowledge base contains two rules: one to check that the field length for a customer's name is greater than or equal to five characters; the other to check for loan amounts less than $10,000. However, these rules are in isolation and are not attached in any way to our operational data set.

The next step is to link up the rules with the data we want them to work on. This is achieved by creating a new **Data Quality Project**:

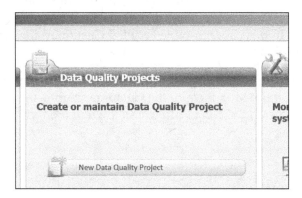

Click on the **New Data Quality Project** button.

Enter a name for the new **Data Quality Project**, and select the knowledge base created earlier, as shown in the following screenshot:

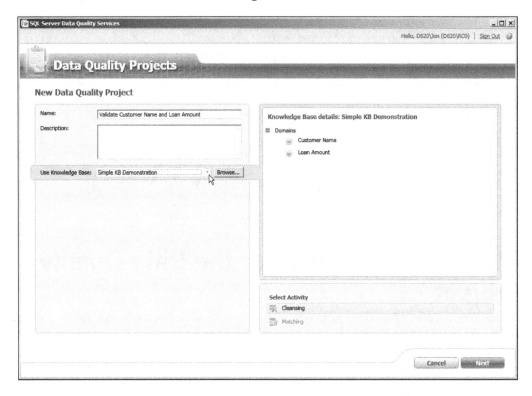

As we can see, the knowledge base contains the **Customer Name** and **Loan Amount** domains we created, along with the rules we defined. Now, click on the Next button and select the **Test** database, where our operational data is stored. Then select the table to be cleansed. In this case our table is called Customer, the table we created at the beginning of this chapter.

In the **Mappings** grid, select the **CustomerName** and **LoanAmount** source columns from the operational data. Map them to the **Customer Name** and **Loan Amount** domains and then click on the **Next** button, as shown in the following screenshot:

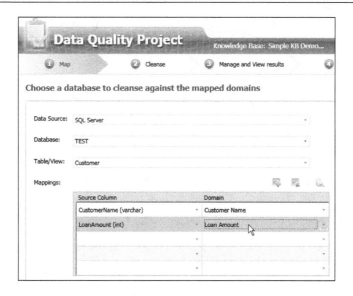

The **Cleanse** screen now appears. Click on the **Start** button to begin the cleansing process. The domain rules that we defined will now be applied to the operational data columns in the table we selected in the previous screenshot. The following screenshot will appear on the right-hand side of the **DQS Profiler** grid:

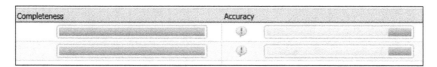

This tells us that all of the records have been processed, but not all of them reach the desired standard of data quality or accuracy. Click on the **Next** button to proceed to the next page and manage the results. We can see that the Customer domain is selected. Click on the **Invalid** tab to view the records that do not match the domain rule we defined for **Customer Name**:

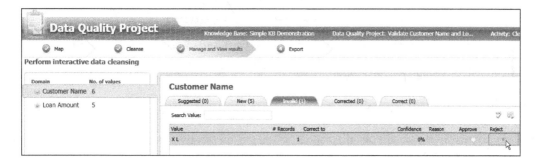

If we now click on the **Approve** button, we are indicating that the rule has found one or more records that are incorrect, and that we "approve" of the choice the rule made. The record is now moved to the **Correct** tab.

Now do the same thing for the **Loan Amount** domain, as shown in the following screenshot:

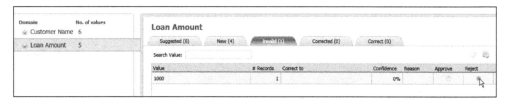

Once approved, we click on the **Next** button to take us to the final stage of the cleansing process. Here, on the left-hand side of the page, we can see a sample of the records that have been processed. However, the interesting part of this page is on the right-hand side. The **Approve** button allows us to export the results to a table (or **Excel/CSV** file), as shown in the following screenshot:

Click on the **Export** button to push the cleansed data out to the SQL Server.

At this stage it is useful to select the **Data and Cleansing Info Output Format** option, as it exports the information that identifies which values in the input data do not obey the rules you have defined.

Identifying invalid records and columns

After the data cleansing has completed, we can run useful queries such as the following, from SQL Server Management Studio:

```
USE Test
go

SELECT    *
FROM      Cleansed_Customer
WHERE     Record_status = 'Invalid'
```

This allows us to quickly identify those records that are invalid. If we want to narrow the choice down to a column type that is invalid, we can do this too. For example, to find invalid customer names, we use the following query:

```
SELECT    *
FROM      Cleansed_Customer
WHERE     CustomerName_status = 'Invalid'
```

DQS versus T-SQL

You may be asking at this point, "Why not do all of this in T-SQL?", and it would be a good question. The short answer is that DQS has the advantage of a knowledge base that can be expanded and shared, and which is decoupled from the data. Although all of the knowledge is in one place, it can be shared among multiple teams that are are working on data quality issues – big data warehouse projects will definitely benefit from this. Furthermore, you don't need T-SQL knowledge to do it, which is great for us DBAs and developers as we don't spend our day writing basic, tedious queries - end users can easily create these for themselves. This means we can finally do the more interesting things that are included in SQL Server 2012.

Having said that, now let us do something a little more complex, such as *replacing values*.

If you still have the DQS client interface open, click on **Finish**. If you have closed DQS, open it up again, and on the left-hand pane, click on the knowledge base we named **Simple KB Demonstration**, and then select **Domain Management**:

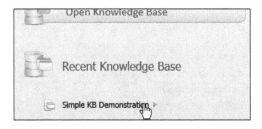

Click on the **Create a domain** button, and this time call the domain **Gender**:

Click on **OK** and you will see the **Domain Management** screen. This time, we will use the **Domain Values** tab to map existing values in the **Sex** column to new and consistent values. We will ensure that any instances of **Female** are changed to **F** and any instances of **Male** are changed to **M**, to make them uniform with other values in the same column. If you have ever written even a basic T-SQL report query, you can probably already see all of those extra OR statements in the WHERE clause dissolving in front of your eyes.

Next, click on the **Add New Domain Value** button as shown in the following screenshot:

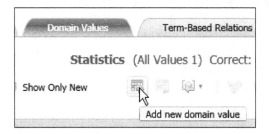

Add the following entry in order to map any occurrences of **Female** to **F**, as shown in the following screenshot:

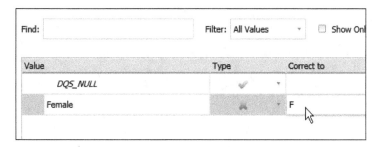

Click **Enter** on your keyboard to complete the entry, and you will notice that an additional entry is added for the **F** column to show that it is correct and does not require mapping, as seen in the following screenshot:

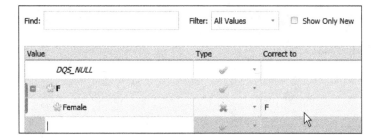

Now click on the **Finish** button and confirm that you would like to publish the knowledge base.

Once completed, click on the **New Data Quality Project** button on the DQS Client front page. You need to do this because you have changed what is being validated, so it constitutes a new project. Name the project Customer, Loan and Gender validation. You can see on the right-hand side that there are now three domains instead of the two we had earlier. Click on the **Next** button and again, select the **Test** database and the **Customer** table, and map the columns to domains, as shown in the following screenshot:

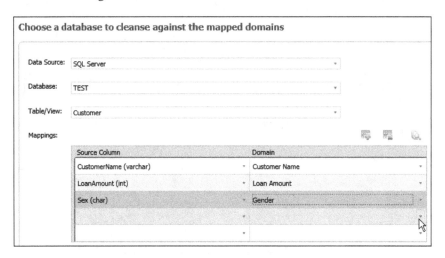

Click on the **Next** button to move to the **Cleanse** page, then on the **Restart** button as shown in the following screenshot. We are nearly finished:

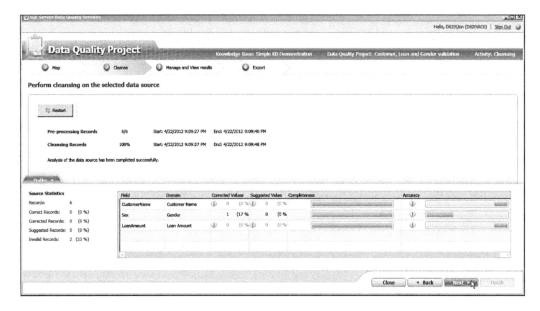

This time around we can see that some of the records have been corrected, specifically those with an incorrect value in the **Sex** column. Once the records have been cleansed, click on the **Next** button, as shown in the following screenshot:

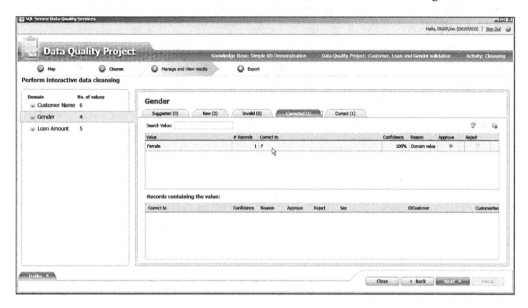

Click on the **Gender** domain on the left-hand side of the results page. Then click on the Corrected tab to show those records that have been changed according to the rules defined for the Gender domain. Note how the value **Female** has now been correctly mapped onto the standardized value **F** in the previous screenshot.

We want to keep this change, so we leave the **Approve** radio button selected and click on the **Next** button to achieve the following output, as shown in the next screenshot:

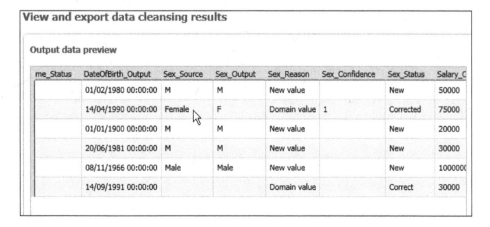

The **Output data preview** grid on the **Export** page confirms that the correction to the data has taken place. Furthermore, it places a value of **Corrected** in the **Sex_Status** column to show that the **Sex** column has been changed on this row. Complete the **Export** panel as shown in the following screenshot, by clicking on the **Export** button, confirming that you wish to overwrite the table:

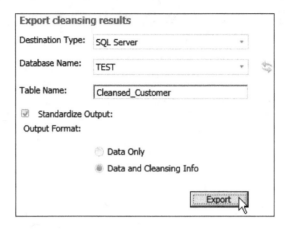

Click on **Finish**, switch to **SQL Server Management Studio** and connect to the **Test** database. Run the following query:

```
SELECT   *
FROM     Cleansed_Customer
```

As shown in the following screenshot, the **Sex_Output** column now has an **F** instead of **Female**, and the **Sex_Status** column has a value of **Corrected**:

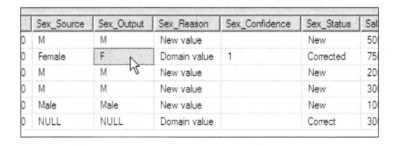

	Sex_Source	Sex_Output	Sex_Reason	Sex_Confidence	Sex_Status	Sal
0	M	M	New value		New	50
0	Female	F	Domain value	1	Corrected	75
0	M	M	New value		New	20
0	M	M	New value		New	30
0	Male	Male	New value		New	10
0	NULL	NULL	Domain value		Correct	30

As DBAs and developers, this is very useful as we can use this information to easily update source systems. The following T-SQL query updates the original data with the corrections DQS found, matching rows based on the ID column and only updating those where the status flag was set to Corrected by DQS:

```
UPDATE  Customer
SET     Customer.Sex = Sex_Output
FROM    Cleansed_Customer
WHERE   Customer.IDCustomer = Cleansed_Customer.IDCustomer_Output
AND     Sex_Status = 'Corrected'

SELECT *
FROM    Customer
```

As shown in the results from the following screenshot, Alice's sex has now changed from **Female** to **F**, conforming to the other entries:

	IDCustomer	CustomerName	DateOfBirth	Sex	Salary	LoanAmount
1	120	John Smith	1980-02-01 00:00:00.000	M	50000	100000
2	130	Alice Jones	1990-04-14 00:00:00.000	F	75000	1000
3	140	Simon Evans	1900-01-01 00:00:00.000	M	20000	25000
4	150	X L	1981-06-20 00:00:00.000	M	30000	50000
5	160	Jim Bob	1966-11-08 00:00:00.000	Male	10000000	25000
6	170	Hilary Smith	1991-09-14 00:00:00.000	NULL	30000	45000

Obviously, this is a basic example, looking at a single value in a single column, which would have been quicker and easier to perform using a T-SQL update query. However, the real power of DQS is two-fold:

Firstly, it allows users without SQL skills to identify and create data cleansing requirements. This moves the task from those who are less familiar with the data (perhaps the DBAs and developers who have the technical but not business knowledge), back to business users who do understand what constitutes valid data.

Secondly, it decouples the validation from the data source. This allows company-wide, or even inter-company, validation rules to be created. These rules can then be mapped to individual data sets as needed, making them reusable for multiple development projects..

 Exercise: Go through the procedure just described, but this time create a rule that will change any entries in the **Sex** column from **Male** to **M**.

Resources

DQS is a powerful new feature in SQL Server 2012 and, like any other feature, there is plenty to explore and even more to learn. The following resources will help you build on the examples you have seen in this book, so that you can begin to use DQS to cleanse your data and increase its accuracy:

Microsoft's DQS page on MSDN can be found at:

`http://msdn.microsoft.com/en-us/library/`
`ff877917(v=sql.110).aspx.`

In addition, the DQS team at Microsoft has created a useful set of tutorial videos, which go into more detail. These can be found at:

`http://msdn.microsoft.com/en-us/sqlserver/hh323832.`

and:

`http://technet.microsoft.com/en-us/sqlserver/hh780961`

Microsoft have also released some basic information about integrating DQS with SSIS for automated data cleansing here:

`msdn.microsoft.com/en-us/library/ee677619.aspx.`

Summary

Data quality, more than ever before, is a pressing issue for organizations. With business intelligence and data mining currently featuring so prominently on the corporate decision-support wish list, data quality underpins useful and accurate decisions.

While we have examined a purposely trivial example here, it serves to illustrate just how powerful DQS can be in an environment with tables that have millions of rows of data and hundreds of tables. With the addition of business procedures and naming conventions, a business data expert can examine the data, create rules to flag data that is invalid, and extract data that is to be changed in order to standardize it across the system.

Once corrections have been identified, the changes to the data can be reviewed to ensure they are correct, and saved as domains in the DQS knowledge base. Finally, the changes can be written out to either a database table or a file. All of this can be done without the ongoing and expensive involvement of a DBA or developer, who now only needs to be involved right at the end of the business data analysis process, in order to make changes to the original data.

DQS is a useful first step to creating standardized, clean business data in SQL Server-based systems, on which reliable decisions can be made with greater confidence. We expect it to evolve rapidly in future editions, alongside its integration with SSIS.

In the next chapter, we will take a look at another big new feature in SQL Server 2012, aimed primarily at production environments—the new high availability feature, AlwaysOn.

8
AlwaysOn

SQL Server 2012 has a multitude of new administrative features. Some of these features, such as AlwaysOn, could have an entire book devoted solely to them. We are not going to go through a full tutorial here, but instead we will take a look at the basics, while throwing in a few tips to give you a flavor of what AlwaysOn involves.

It should be noted that AlwaysOn is very much a marketing term, which simply encompasses availability groups and clustering. It seems to be a common misconception that availability groups have replaced SQL Server mirroring, but they have not. If you don't need availability groups, nor wish to introduce the complexity of clusters into your environment, mirroring is still available to you, just as it was in SQL Server 2008. However, read on, as this situation will eventually change.

Mirroring, clustering and availability groups

Take a seat, put down any hot drinks and prepare to be shocked: mirroring has been deprecated. This may come as quite a jolt to anyone who reads it, as it did to us, the authors. To use a more accurate SQL Profiler term, mirroring has been marked for deprecation. This means it will almost certainly still be available for the next two editions of SQL Server. In practice, it is probably going to be close to 2020 by the time we have to worry about it. By this time, availability groups should be as good, if not better than mirroring, in every sense.

There is a perception that availability groups replace clustering, but this is not the case. Clustering allows failover at the SQL Server instance level, whereas availability groups fail over at the database level. However, availability groups do employ the services of **Windows Server Failover Clustering (WSFC),** quite simply because it made more sense to use a technology that was tried and tested, rather than rewrite code that is already part of Windows.

The other advantage of utilizing Windows Server Failover Clustering is that availability groups and clustering work better together, as they share the same technology, whereas database mirroring and clustering don't work so well, because they operate independently.

So if you still want to have the high availability advantages of a cluster with mirroring, availability groups are a much better and more reliable option, and require less DBA intervention when the pressure is on.

Availability groups

Availability groups are what were referred to in the beta phase of SQL Server 2012 as **HA/DR or HADRON (High Availability/Disaster Recovery/AlwaysOn)**. That has now passed and *AlwaysOn Availability Groups* is the new phrase. Think of availability groups as a better, more reliable version of database mirroring, but replace the idea of a database mirror with the word replica. Before we go into the details, let us take a quick look at the pros and cons of availability groups.

Availability group restrictions

There are certain restrictions imposed upon availability groups:

- Both SQL Server 2012 Enterprise Edition and Windows Server 2008 (R2) Enterprise Edition are required to take advantage of availability groups. There is no functionality for availability groups in the Standard or BI editions of SQL Server 2012.

- To implement availability groups a Windows Server Failover Cluster will need to be set up first. At present this is for Windows Server 2008 and 2008 R2 only, but availability groups can be set up on Windows 8 Server when it is released.

- A database can be a member of only one availability group.

- Differential backups cannot be made from a replica.

- Full backups have to be made as a *Copy Only* on replicas.

- System databases cannot form part of an availability group.

- To deploy mirroring or AlwaysOn, the database must be in *Full Recovery* mode. A database in *Simple Recovery* mode *cannot* be used.

Availability group advantages

- In a disaster recovery (DR) situation, you can now specify that groups of databases fail over as one group, rather than individually. This substantially eases the DBA burden.

- Availability groups are appropriate in situations where applications need access to multiple databases in order to function in full. A good example is the Membership database in an ASP.NET application, which is used to securely log in users. It needs a connection to other databases, such as Products, Customers, Finance and so on in order to work. If one database comes online before the others, it is of no use until they have all failed over.

- By using availability groups you can failover your databases together, ensuring certain users or applications are up and working with others that interact with them at the application level.

- In addition to the primary database, four mirrors, or *replicas*, as they should now be referred to, can be created.

- Up to two synchronous replicas can be created, though the remaining two must be asynchronous if they are implemented.

- Read-only queries can be run from either synchronous or asynchronous replicas in real time; there is no longer a need for database snapshots or connections to be dropped.

> Mirror servers that were previously idle, consuming power and not doing much else, can now be used as read-only, up-to-date copies of the main production database server, without the need to take periodic snapshots, which become quickly out of date.
>
> This is ideal for running reports against without hitting the main OLTP system. However, don't under-specify the replica servers, especially if they are running synchronously. Make sure tempdb is on a fast drive by itself, as it is used heavily to reduce contention between transactions being written to the replica, and queries being run against it.

- Multiple user databases can be mirrored in an availability group relationship. This allows them to be failed over as a single atomic group, in the same way that a resource group can currently be failed over in a Windows failover clustering scenario.

- Full or transaction log backups can be made from a database replica. Note that as full backups can only be made as *Copy Only*, they do not break the log chain.

> For performance and efficiency, run a full or transaction log backup against the secondary database, taking the load off the production server.

- Failover times are improved over mirroring.

- In terms of failover granularity, availability groups fit into the gap between mirroring, where the failover unit is a single database, and clustering, where the failover unit is the entire SQL Server instance. This allows all of the databases that belong to a single application to be failed over in unison which, from a business continuity and DBA workload perspective, is definitely the way to go.

- There is a new health detection feature available for SQL Server, which is used for shared disk as well as non-shared disk deployments.

Using availability groups

As availability groups essentially extend the idea of mirroring, many of the current concepts you are already familiar with if you have been using mirroring apply equally to availability groups, so the learning curve is minimal. Once you have set up the Windows and SQL Server cluster and created your endpoints between two SQL Server instances, you need do only a few new things to put an availability group in place.

But before you do anything else, you will need to configure your SQL Server 2012 instance to have the AlwaysOn functionality enabled. This can be done by opening **SQL Server Configuration Manager**, selecting the **SQL Server Services** node, and right-clicking on the SQL Server instance for which you wish to enable AlwaysOn. Then select **Properties** and click on the **AlwaysOn High Availability** tab to enable it.

To make use of AlwaysOn, you need to be running the Enterprise Edition of SQL Server 2012, and it must run on Windows Server 2008 (or later versions) with the Windows Server Failover Cluster 2494036 hotfix applied first. Once this is installed and set up, the difficult part is over and the fun begins.

To create an availability group, use the following T-SQL statement:

```
CREATE AVAILABILITY GROUP PRODUCTION
FOR DATABASE CRMDB
REPLICA ON

'DRSERVER1' WITH
(
    AVAILABILITY_MODE = SYNCHRONOUS_COMMIT
)
,
'DRSERVER2' WITH
(
    AVAILABILITY_MODE = ASYNCHRONOUS_COMMIT
)
```

Note that we have specified two DR servers here to hold the replicas. You can specify anything from one to four secondary replicas. Just like mirroring, a replica can be synchronous or asynchronous. But the great thing about AlwaysOn is that you can mix and match according to your availability and recovery needs, just as in the previous example.

Familiarize yourself with the WITH clause of the CREATE AVAILABILITY GROUP command. It is very powerful and allows you to define things such as the failover mode, how backups are taken, timeout periods and whether connections are allowed to the secondary replica. For more details check out TechNet at: http://technet.microsoft.com/en-us/library/ff878399%28SQL.110%29.aspx.

Adding a principal database to an availability group on the primary server is as easy as running the following code:

```
ALTER AVAILABILITY GROUP PRODUCTION
ADD DATABASE CRMDB
```

Be aware that you cannot add a system database to an availability group.

If you accidentally add the wrong primary database, or you add the right database to the wrong availability group, use the following to remove it:

```
ALTER AVAILABILITY GROUP PRODUCTION
REMOVE DATABASE CRMDB
```

You can remove several primary databases from an availability group in a single statement, using the following as an example:

```
ALTER AVAILABILITY GROUP PRODUCTION
REMOVE DATABASE CRMDB1, CRMDB2, CRMDB3
```

Preparing a secondary database is a process similar to that required for creating a mirror.

To deploy mirroring or AlwaysOn, the database *must* be in **Full Recovery** mode. A database in **Simple Recovery** mode *cannot* be used.

First, ensure that a backup of the principal database is available on the primary server in addition to any log backups, if the full backup you are using has been taken overnight. Remember to take a backup of the tail of the log too, as the last scheduled log backup may have occurred some time ago.

Next, copy the database backup from the principal server to the secondary server.

Then restore the database in a non-recovered mode on the secondary server, using the following code:

```
RESTORE DATABASE CRMDB
FROM DISK = 'D:\BACKUPS\CRMDB.bak'
WITH NORECOVERY
```

Note that you can use the WITH MOVE clause at this point if the disk layout on your secondary server is different to that of the principal.

> Keep the disk and folder layout of your principal and secondary servers identical. This makes your life as a DBA easier and generally makes recovery less complex and quicker, especially if you use multiple file groups.

Finally, take any log backups from the principal server and restore them, again leaving the database in a non-recoverable state:

```
RESTORE LOG CRMDB
FROM DISK = 'D:\BACKUPS\CRMDB.trn'
WITH NORECOVERY
```

On the replica server, open up Management Studio and join the server to the availability group:

```
ALTER AVAILABILITY GROUP PRODUCTION JOIN
```

Then, make the secondary database on the replica server a part of the group:

```
ALTER AVAILABILITY GROUP PRODUCTION
ADD REPLICA ON 'DBSERVER1'
WITH (ENDPOINT_URL = 'TCP://DBSERVER1.company.com:7022)
```

Once the secondary database is part of the availability group, its status can be altered using the ALTER DATABASE command. For instance, to remove the replica database from the availability group, run the following query on the secondary database server:

```
ALTER DATABASE CRMDB
SET HADR AVAILABILITY GROUP = OFF
```

This can be useful if the connection to a replica server has broken and the mirroring to the database has fallen far behind. The database can simply be removed from the group and then restored from a fresh backup from the primary database, before reintroducing it to the availability group.

Just like mirroring, availability groups support the automatic page repair functionality from SQL Server 2008. This means that any corrupt pages found on the principal database will attempt a repair with a non-corrupt page from the secondary (or replica) database. The msdb database still contains the *suspect_pages* table, which tracks corrupted pages in any database regardless of its mirroring or availability group status.

> The SQL Server team has included the new DMV **sys.dm_hadr_auto_page_repair** for tracking suspect pages in databases that are part of an availability group. This is identical in its output to the DMV that was available in SQL Server 2008 for mirroring (**sys.dm_db_mirroring_auto_page_repair**), which still exists for mirrored databases in SQL Server 2012. If you have a job or monitoring tool that utilizes a custom query on the original DMV and decide to utilize availability groups, you can easily UNION the two together so that suspect pages can be reported across both mirrors and replicas in a single query.

There is far more to learn about AlwaysOn Availability Groups than we can show you here, but don't be afraid to start investigating the subject further. Setting up the cluster is the difficult part, but it is much easier than it used to be. In addition, the requirements for creating a cluster are less demanding than in previous editions of SQL Server and Windows Server. We highly encourage you to explore it. An extended, high-level overview of its full capabilities is available at http://msdn.microsoft.com/en-us/library/hh781257.aspx.

Summary

In this chapter, we examined the improvement to high availability that AlwaysOn provides. Then we looked at the advantages and disadvantages of availability groups and some of the commands used to administer them. We think this feature is one of the most compelling reasons to upgrade to this new version of SQL Server.

In the next chapter, we will look at the new Distributed Replay feature and how to install, configure, and use it.

9
Distributed Replay

SQL Server has included the ability to replay a trace captured in SQL Server Profiler for quite some time. This feature allows us to run a real-life transactional load against a test or development server, which is useful for simulation purposes.

However, the Achilles' heel of this ability has been that it has only been possible to replay the trace from a single machine, thereby capping its scalability. This limits the usefulness of the tool as it cannot realistically simulate heavy, mission critical loads. In turn, this means you don't always receive meaningful results.

Thankfully, this is not the case anymore. In SQL Server 2012, Microsoft introduces Distributed Replay. This allows DBAs to run that load concurrently from up to 6 client machines. If you are thinking "only 16?", then how about 16 clients x 512 threads per client, or over 8,000 concurrent connections on the Enterprise Edition of SQL Server 2012? This is a very useful feature indeed, not only for load testing, but also for evaluating applications before upgrading to SQL Server 2012; it can also prove beneficial prior to hardware and Windows upgrades. Therefore, because you can now simulate a load coming from multiple clients instead of just one, you can have more confidence that when you upgrade or roll out, everything will work. If it does not, at least you will know before it affects your users and you can investigate without impacting those concerned.

If you are a DBA, a capacity planner, a database architect, or responsible for your development servers, then Distributed Replay is well worth knowing about.

Terminology

Distributed Replay introduces some new terminology. Knowing what this refers to helps to understand what it is about, so let's dive in.

Distributed Replay

Distributed Replay as a concept comprises several parts: two Windows services (the **Distributed Replay Controller** and the **Distributed Replay Client**), the DReplay executable command (sometimes referred to as the **DRU – Distributed Replay Utility**) , and its associated configuration files.

Trace file

The **trace file** is a standard SQL Server Profiler trace file. It is produced by running SQL Server Profiler, typically against a live source server, and is used as the input to a Distributed Replay session.

Intermediate file

The **intermediate file** is produced by processing a SQL Server Profiler trace file using the **DReplay** preprocess command. The file is then used by Distributed Replay to re-create transactions.

Controller

The **Distributed Replay Controller** reads transactions from the intermediate file. It then dispatches the transactions to the clients specified in the **DReplay** command's -w parameter. The clients then replay the transactions against the target server.

Client

A **Distributed Replay Client** is one or more machines that handle the replay of transactions sent from the **Distributed Replay Controller** server, from the intermediate file. By default, each client can run up to 255 threads against the target server, up to a maximum 512 threads per client. It is also worth noting that while the Enterprise Edition of SQL Server 2012 supports up to 16 client machines, all of the other editions, including the Developer Edition, only support one client. Express Edition cannot be used as a Distributed Replay client.

Target

The target is the SQL Server against which the Distributed Replay Client server runs the transactions sent by the controller. This may be a test or development SQL Server database server, or a new server being assessed for capacity planning purposes.

DReplay

DReplay is the main user interface to Distributed Replay. It is executed by the DBAor developer from the command line and has four main options:

```
DREPLAY      preprocess

DREPLAY      replay

DREPLAY      status

DREPLAY      cancel
```

Typically, the DReplay command resides in C:\Program Files (x86)\Microsoft SQL Server\110\Tools\Binn.

This path is included in the environment path variable when Distributed Replay is installed, so you should be able to run DReplay from any location without specifying the full path.

Architecture

Any, or all, of the Distributed Replay components can exist on one, or more than one, server. The configuration will depend on hardware availability and how many users you want to simulate using the replay environment.

Distributed Replay – a hands on example

For the purpose of the following example, we will run everything on a single machine, but in practice (and to make use of the distributed part of Distributed Replay) you would usually employ two or more clients, which is the whole point of it! However, the principles and commands involved are identical, whichever way the system is architected.

Installation

Run setup.exe from the SQL Server 2012 installation media and select the
Distributed Replay Client and **Distributed Replay Controller** options:

```
        □ Analysis Services
        □ Reporting Services - Native
Shared Features
        □ Reporting Services - SharePoint
        □ Reporting Services Add-in for SharePoint Products
        □ Data Quality Client
        □ SQL Server Data Tools
        □ Client Tools Connectivity
        □ Integration Services
        □ Client Tools Backwards Compatibility
        □ Client Tools SDK
        □ Documentation Components
        ☑ Management Tools - Basic
            ☑ Management Tools - Complete
        ☑ Distributed Replay Controller
        ☑ Distributed Replay Client
        ☑ SQL Client Connectivity SDK
        □ Master Data Services
Redistributable Features
```

 If you are running the clients and/or controllers on separate machines,
remember that you may need to open up Windows firewall to allow
connections between machines. Microsoft has published instructions
on how to do this at: http://technet.microsoft.com/en-us/
library/gg502645.aspx.

Next, specify the name of the machine that is to be the **Distributed Replay
Controller**. This is an optional parameter and the default value is blank:

```
Specify controller machine name and directory locations.

Controller Name:    D620

Working Directory:  C:\Program Files (x86)\Microsoft SQL Server\DReplayClient\WorkingDir\

Result Directory:   C:\Program Files (x86)\Microsoft SQL Server\DReplayClient\ResultDir\
```

If you are installing the controller on a different server, enter the name of the
machine, noting the following:

- The **Controller Name** must be a **fully qualified domain name (FQDN)**, unless it is the same machine that the client runs on, in which case the short name can be used, as shown in the previous screenshot.

- If the controller is not yet set up, leave the controller name blank and manually enter it later in the client configuration file.

- Finally, you need to specify which users will have Distributed Replay Controller access and specify their NT login. Note that neither local nor domain (**NT** or **AD – Active Directory**) group accounts can be used, nor any of the built-in accounts. See Microsoft's page at `http://technet. microsoft.com/en-us/library/gg471548`.

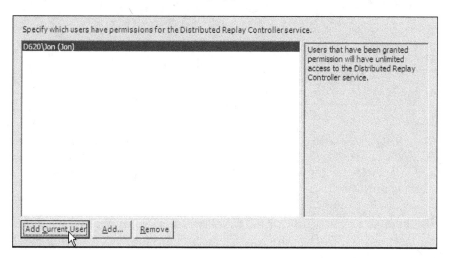

Usage

As soon as you know how to use Distributed Replay, it is surprisingly easy. Although there is no GUI tool as yet, there are four straightforward steps to have it up and running. We will learn how to use it in the following example.

Capture

The capture step is not an integral part of Distributed Replay. Instead, SQL Server Profiler is used to produce a trace file, a concept familiar to most DBAs and many developers.

However, be aware that certain columns need to be captured during the trace in order for the trace file to be used with Distributed Replay. These can be set up manually, but there is an easier way. Open **SQL Server Profiler** and connect to the database server from which you want to create the trace. Select the options shown in the following screenshot, and then click on the **Run** button:

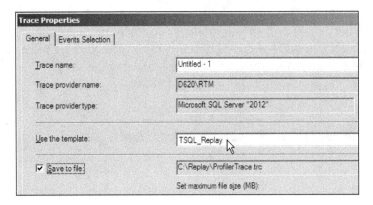

 TSQL_Replay has been chosen as the trace template. Here, the output file has been created in C:\Replay\ProfilerTrace.trc to keep this example straightforward, but it would normally be placed elsewhere in practice.

Of course, if you are testing this for the first time, it is useful to have a script that will create sample SQL DML (Data Manipulation Language) commands that can be replayed. Here is the code:

```
USE tempdb
GO

IF NOT EXISTS
(SELECT name FROM sysobjects WHERE name = 'tblDistRepTest')

CREATE TABLE tblDistRepTest
(RowNo int, TimeAdded datetime default GETDATE())

DECLARE @i int
SET @i=0

WHILE      @i < 30
BEGIN
```

```
SET @i = @i + 1

INSERT INTO tblDistRepTest (RowNo)
VALUES (@i)

WAITFOR DELAY '00:00:02'

END


SELECT * FROM tblDistRepTest
```

For the purpose of understanding Distributed Replay, run the SQL commands shown in the previous code (or write some of your own to perform inserts, updates or deletes). In a real-world situation, you would usually run the trace against a production server. However, this is best performed with SQL Profiler running on a different machine in order to reduce load on the production server.

After the script has finished running and you have a profiler trace file, stop the trace and close SQL Profiler. Finally, execute the following query to drop the table created earlier:

```
DROP TABLE tblDistRepTest
```

This must be done so that later on we can verify that the replay has worked. Now we can move on to the next step.

Preprocess

Preprocessing is a fancy term that just means *convert*. Preprocessing is required because the format that SQL Profiler produces for trace files cannot be used directly by Distributed Replay. Instead, we have to manually preprocess the trace file into the intermediate format required by Distributed Replay. Fortunately, this is a one-time operation for each trace we create, unless we want to change the system it will be replayed on.

To do this, open a DOS command box and type the following:

```
DREPLAY preprocess -i "c:\Replay\ProfilerTrace.trc"  -d "c:\Replay"
```

-i specifies the input file, which is a SQL Server Profiler trace file.

-d is the location of the folder in which the intermediate file will be written.

The converted file, generated by DReplay is always called ReplayEvents.irf.

If you receive an error message whilst attempting to create the intermediate file stating that you cannot connect to the controller, start the Windows Services console (`services.msc`) and check that the **SQL Server Distributed Replay Controller** service is running:

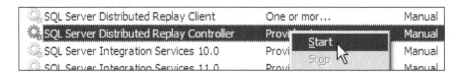

If the directory specified in the -d option does not exist, it will be created automatically. Observe that another file, `TraceStats.xml` is also written into the folder. This contains interesting information about the original trace file, including connection information, the number of SPIDs and the number of events related to each SPID.

Once the intermediate file has been created, output similar to the following screenshot should be seen. We can then move on to the next step of replaying it.

```
C:\Windows\System32>dreplay preprocess -m D620 -i "c:\Replay\ProfilerTrace.trc" -d "c:\Replay"
2012-05-11 14:32:59:665 Info DReplay     Preprocessing pass 1 of 2 in progress.
2012-05-11 14:33:00:473 Info DReplay     Preprocessing pass 1 of 2 completed.
2012-05-11 14:33:00:473 Info DReplay     Preprocessing pass 2 of 2 in progress.
2012-05-11 14:33:00:475 Info DReplay     Preprocessing pass 2 of 2 completed.
2012-05-11 14:33:00:482 Info DReplay     11 replayable events written to intermediate file in c:\Replay.
2012-05-11 14:33:00:490 Info DReplay     Elapsed time: 0 day(s), 0 hour(s), 0 minute(s), 1 second(s).
```

Replay

The interesting work begins when replaying the intermediate file against the target server. We can do this from the command line using the following instructions:

```
DREPLAY replay
-s TARGETSERVER\INSTANCE
-w CLIENT1, CLIENT2,....,CLIENTn
-m D620
-d "c:\Replay"
```

For clarity, in the previous example, each parameter is shown on a separate line in, but in reality they just need to be separated by a single space.

-s specifies against which server the intermediate trace file will be replayed. This can be a base SQL Server installation, or a secondary instance, such as `Server\InstanceName`.

-w is a comma delimited list of clients that will replay the intermediate trace file.

-m is the name of the Distributed Replay Controller server.

-d is the name of the folder containing the intermediate file created in the preprocess step.

> Unusually for Windows, it is important to note that the DReplay flags are case sensitive.
>
> There are other replay options, but those we have used here are the most useful. However, should you wish to explore them, run the following code:
>
> ```
> DREPLAY replay -?
> ```

If you receive the message **The client is not a registered Distributed Replay Client**, you may need to start the **SQL Server Distributed Replay Client** service as shown in the following screenshot, and ensure there are no firewall issues:

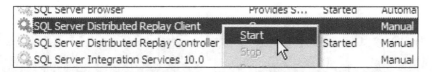

In this case, take a look at the ReplayResult.trc file, which can be found in `C:\Program Files (x86)\Microsoft SQL Server\110\Tools\DReplayClient\ResultDir`.

Double click the `ReplayResult.trc` file to open it in SQL Profiler and troubleshoot the problem, as shown in the following screenshot:

EventClass	EventSequence	ReplaySequence	TextData
Replay Settings Event			<?xml version="1.0" encoding="UTF-16"?> <ReplaySettings> <ReplayTarget>D620\RTM</ReplayTarget> <Ser
Replay Provider Error	744	3	Login failed for user 'NT Service\SQL Server Distributed Replay Client'.
Audit Login	744	3	-- network protocol: LPC set quoted_identifier on set arithabort off set numeric_roundabort off
Replay Provider Error	746	5	Login failed for user 'NT Service\SQL Server Distributed Replay Client'.
Audit Login	746	5	-- network protocol: LPC set quoted_identifier on set arithabort on set numeric_roundabort off
Replay Provider Error	743	2	Login failed for user 'NT Service\SQL Server Distributed Replay Client'.
Audit Login	743	2	-- network protocol: LPC set quoted_identifier off set arithabort off set numeric_roundabort off

As we can see, the reason the trace has failed, is because the service account that the Distributed Replay Client server requires, has not been added as a login to the SQL Server on which the intermediate file is being replayed.

Always add the Distributed Replay Client service account as an NT/ Active Directory login to the target SQL Server, even on a standalone machine. If in doubt, you may very *cautiously* wish to consider granting it SQL Server sysadmin rights to avoid any problems during replay. Do this with caution, as the target server should only be a development or test box, or a server which has not yet been commissioned into the production environment. Always drop or disable the account afterwards to ensure it cannot be used accidentally and without forethought.

In addition, remember that the account(s) that originally ran the queries on the server, on which the initial trace was created, must also exist with the same permissions on the server on which the trace is replayed.

We have now added the Distributed Replay service account and re-run the replay. This time the output should look like the following screenshot, with a 100 percent pass rate:

```
C:\Windows\System32>dreplay replay -s D620\RTM -w D620 -m D620 -d "c:\Replay"
2012-05-11 14:45:02:250 Info  DReplay    Dispatching in progress.
2012-05-11 14:45:02:258 Info  DReplay    0 events have been dispatched.
2012-05-11 14:45:03:455 Info  DReplay    Dispatching has completed.
2012-05-11 14:45:03:456 Info  DReplay    11 events dispatched in total.
2012-05-11 14:45:03:459 Info  DReplay    Elapsed time: 0 day(s), 0 hour(s), 0 minute(s), 0 second(s).
2012-05-11 14:45:03:460 Info  DReplay    Event replay in progress.
2012-05-11 14:45:33:467 Info  DReplay    D620: 5 events replayed, 5 events succeeded (pass rate 100.00 %).
2012-05-11 14:45:33:469 Info  DReplay    5 events (45.45 %) have been replayed. Estimated time remaining: 37 second(s).
2012-05-11 14:45:41:057 Info  DReplay    Event replay has completed.
2012-05-11 14:45:41:059 Info  DReplay    11 events (100 %) have been replayed in total. Pass rate 100.00 %.
2012-05-11 14:45:41:061 Info  DReplay    Elapsed time: 0 day(s), 0 hour(s), 0 minute(s), 39 second(s).

C:\Windows\System32>
```

If you need to repeatedly re-run a Distributed Replay file, put the DReplay replay command into a .bat or .cmd file.

As everything has run successfully, we should now be able to reconnect to SQL Server from Management Studio and run a SELECT query against the previously dropped table:

```
SELECT * FROM tblDistRepTest
```

We should see the result set with the current timestamp, as shown in the following screenshot:

	RowNo	TimeAdded
1	1	2012-05-11 21:29:53.580
2	2	2012-05-11 21:29:54.580
3	3	2012-05-11 21:29:55.580
4	4	2012-05-11 21:29:56.580
5	5	2012-05-11 21:29:57.580
6	6	2012-05-11 21:29:58.580
7	7	2012-05-11 21:29:59.580
8	8	2012-05-11 21:30:00.580
9	9	2012-05-11 21:30:01.607
10	10	2012-05-11 21:30:02.607
11	11	2012-05-11 21:30:03.607
12	12	2012-05-11 21:30:04.607

Great! We have run a successful replay and created a new table with data to confirm this. Now we can gather query timings and compare the results across servers. We recommend that timings for any operations you wish to compare are included in the code rather than monitoring them on screen. This way, the timings will be more accurate, can be stored for future use, and will exclude the setup periods introduced by Distributed Replay.

Configuration

Apart from the command-line flags, there are two configuration files you need to know about. These can both be found in C:\Program Files (x86)\Microsoft SQL Server\110\Tools\Binn, and can be safely opened in Notepad or viewed in a web browser.

DReplay.Exe.Preprocess.config is used to configure the generation of intermediate files when the DReplay preprocess command is invoked. It is not usually a necessity to alter this file.

DReplay.Exe.Replay.config is much more useful. This determines how the intermediate trace file is replayed by the controller against the replay clients. It is read by the DReplay command, just before the intermediate file is replayed.

There are nine configuration options, of which the following are most likely to be useful in a capacity planning or load testing exercise:

- `SequencingMode`: This value can be set to either "stress" or "synchronization". Stress is useful for capacity planning and load forecasting, as it drives the replayed transactions against the server as fast as possible, without time-based synchronization of transactions across connections. Synchronization mode is more useful for application compatibility testing and performance testing, as it maintains the synchronization of transactions across connections.

- `StressScaleGranularity`: This is used in conjunction with SequencingMode, which is set to "stress". It takes a value of "SPID" or "Connection" to determine if the connections on a SPID should be scaled as if they were a single SPID, or as individual connections.

- `ThinkTimeScale`: This is a value between 1 and 100. It represents the "user" think time between transactions. It is a percentage, so 100 means 100 percent or "real" user think time. Smaller values speed up the replay speed.

- `ThreadsPerClient`: This defaults to 255, but can be set to integer values between 1 and 512. It determines how many processing threads will be used on each of the replay clients in order to replay the trace.

Monitoring

How do we know that our Distributed Replay is running without problems? We use the `DReplay` status command. This can be run as follows, from the controller server:

```
DREPLAY status
```

Alternatively, the controller can be specified explicitly if run from another server:

```
DREPLAY status -m controllername
```

There is another useful option that can be combined with either of the previous code examples, which specifies how frequently the status is updated. For instance, to update the status every 10 seconds use:

```
DREPLAY status -f 10
```

Or use:

```
DREPLAY status -f 10 -m controllername
```

Canceling

A Distributed Replay session can be cancelled at any time by invoking the cancel command. This is done as follows:

```
DREPLAY cancel
```

The cancel command can be run without any parameters, and it will cancel the running of a replay file on the controller on the local machine. Note that it may take a short time to take effect.

If you want to cancel the replay on a different machine, use the following syntax:

```
DREPLAY cancel  -m controllername
```

If you are planning on running this as part of a script, the -q (quiet) option is useful, as it suppresses the prompt to the user when the cancel command is executed:

```
DREPLAY cancel  -q
```

Or:

```
DREPLAY cancel  -q      -m controller
```

Additional resources

We recommend you read the instructions from Microsoft that show you how to prepare your trace file, replay it and then analyze the results:

```
http://technet.microsoft.com/en-us/library/ff878183%28SQL.110%29.aspx.
```

Microsoft's Jamie Westover has written an article titled "Installing the Distributed Replay Utility", which you can find at:

```
http://social.technet.microsoft.com/wiki/contents/articles/
installing-the-distributed-replay-utility.aspx.
```

Summary

In this chapter we explored the reasons why the Distributed Replay tool is a useful addition to the SQL Server DBA and developer's toolkit. We walked through the steps required to install and configure it, and highlighted some of the potential problems you may encounter. Then we looked at how to use it by creating and replaying a trace file. It is worth becoming familiar with Distributed Replay so you can reap the benefits in your work. We think it is a great addition to SQL Server.

In the final chapter, we will look at SQL Azure and how it may affect you as a developer or DBA. We will also take a look at big data and learn about something that Microsoft are about to release on the Windows platform, namely, Hadoop.

10
Big Data and the Cloud

Back in the first half of the 1990s, SQL Server was supplied on four floppy disks. Later, it migrated to CD. Today, it can be downloaded or ordered on DVD. SQL Server has moved on, not only in how it is delivered to us, but also where it resides after it has been installed. It has grown from a better-than-Access database on nothing more than desktop PCs, to a truly corporate, enterprise-standard relational platform that consistently out-performs the competition in the latest Transaction Processing Council (TPC) speed tests - see the link at the bottom of this page. SQL Server is now one of the big players.

There are two major and immediate challenges ahead for SQL Server, which in turn present challenges for us as SQL Server professionals. The first challenge is the cloud — cynics might claim this is merely hosting on a large scale, a marketing exercise applied to the old computer bureau services of the 1970s. True, cloud is an outsourced hosted service, but it offers more than that, as we will discover in this chapter.

The second challenge is "big data" — the current buzz word in data and database circles. Big data deals with just that - very large quantities of data that simply cannot be handled easily or cost effectively using traditional methods. Yet it is more than that. We will explore how Microsoft intends to deal with this, and cut through the marketing gloss to uncover how it might impact us.

 TPC-E Top Ten Performance Results, Version 1, 21-Jul-2012 available at: `http://www.tpc.org/tpce/results/tpce_perf_results.asp`.

Measure twice, cut once

Like many new concepts, both cloud computing and big data are subjects of some overhyped claims that sometimes border on disbelief. We have attempted to eliminate the hype in order to present a level-headed and objective discussion about these new SQL Server features, without making over-inflated claims or unwarranted criticism. Our advice would be to educate yourself, and back up any assumptions with research and prototypes before you commit serious business funds to either.

SQL Azure: SQL Server in the cloud

What is the cloud? To put it in basic terms, it means that an external company hosts your databases on the servers in their data center, supported by their staff.

Why would we want someone else to have responsibility for our data, with all the risks, such as security, that it encompasses? As is often the case, it is about the bottom line and the potential cost savings of such a service. Fundamentally, you are buying software as a service (SaaS). Paying for a service is a direct, non-taxable cost to the business and is considered an expense in most countries. This is known as operational expenditure, a service cost just like a gas or electricity utility bill. Your finance people probably refer to it as OPEX – operational expenditure.

Your company accountant can probably tell you that OPEX is going to cost far less in tax than CAPEX – capital expenditure. Servers, SANs, network equipment and physical hardware all incur taxes and support costs, OPEX items don't.

What this means for DBAs and developers is that in times of austerity and cutbacks, ways will be sought to reduce costs and taxes in order to free up money to invest in other areas of the business that generate profit. More profit usually means safer jobs, which is a good thing. Therefore we should familiarize ourselves with SQL Azure, as it may be imposed upon us.

Reasons for migrating to the cloud

Now that you know the business reason to migrate to SQL Azure, what do you need to know in technical terms before you can use it? Placing SQL Server in the cloud has a number of advantages. First, it is scalable so you can add more processing power to your database server as needed, and just in time. In order to provide scalability, federations are used, where tables can be shared based on a key ID value, across multiple databases. Second, it is highly available with multiple background instances and automatic failover. Third, it takes the mundane aspects of day-to-day administration out of your hands, allowing you to work on more interesting aspects of SQL Server.

SQL Azure suitability

If there is one piece of advice we would offer, it would be to do your research before signing up for SQL Azure. SQL Azure is not an answer to every database problem. While some applications are suitable for SQL Azure, some simply *cannot* be migrated because of their architecture. As a guideline, it is currently most suited to average-sized database applications, created in-house, which don't rely on anything other than the core database platform functionality. So where should we *not* use it??

- Any system where statutory regulations apply and prevent the database being moved to another jurisdiction for information privacy, sanction, or tax regulations. *If you even suspect that the data in your databases is subject to any of these rules, check this first,* as a little due diligence and bad news upfront, can save a lot of money in fines (and even prison sentences!) further down the line.

- In databases larger than 150 GB; for instance, data warehouses.

- For applications that are CPU or memory intensive, such as simulation software. At present, SQL Azure limits memory consumption to 14GB and 8 x 1.4 GHz processors, which is simply not enough for some categories of application, though undoubtedly this will increase in the future.

- Mission critical systems, requiring an uptime SLA greater than 99.9 percent.

- For third-party applications that may have specific requirements, which only the vendor can change due to support agreements.

- In any system that uses backup and restore jobs, Service Broker, CLR functions, change data capture (CDC), Open XML, or XML indexes.

How SQL Azure differs from hosted web and database services

With a hosted database service, you are provided with the hardware, OS, and database platform. After that, you are on your own. You are responsible for high availability and failover, and may or may not be responsible for backups. But you do have the freedom to do pretty much what you like with it, including adding in external CLR modules, performing backups to your own schedule, and even choosing the type of RAID setup in some cases.

With SQL Azure, much of this is taken away from you, especially the high availability aspects. You are not allowed to change default server-level settings such as collations and sort orders, use trace flags, or distributed transactions, nor can you choose data file placements, use global temporary tables or system tables. Furthermore, it is not advisable to use features marked for deprecation (but not yet deprecated).

A list of supported and unsupported SQL Azure T-SQL commands can be found at: `http://msdn.microsoft.com/en-us/library/windowsazure/ee336250`.

Differences between a public and private cloud

Public cloud services are run by companies such as Microsoft or Amazon and are suited to small to medium sized databases, which have typical, non-specialist requirements.

A **private cloud** can be hosted either in your own data center, or by a specialist company. We know of at least one global company that provides niche market, predictive analysis software to the insurance industry, which is taking this route. What is the reason for this? Their software relies on massive, highly detailed datasets, which require extensive number crunching. For their smaller customers, this means investing in high-end, 48-core servers with a minimum of 256GB of RAM. This is obviously a very large outlay and one that is only used for perhaps 40 hours per week. This kind of application is ideally suited to cloud computing, where it can be provided as SaaS, with the hardware investment picked up by the vendor and utilized to its maximum extent, 24 x 7, around the globe.

Migrating a database to SQL Azure

You may be surprised at how easy it is to migrate to SQL Azure; create an account at the `SQLAzure.com` website, migrate your schema, and then migrate the data using the following steps:

1. Sign up for an account at `SQLAzure.com` (this directs you to the Windows Azure website). Make a note of your login details and the server name allocated to you.

2. Connect to SQL Azure and create a new database using either SQL Server Management Studio or SQL Server Data Tools, just as you would on a local server or PC.

3. Next, script out all of the database objects from the source database, by right-clicking on the database and selecting **Tasks...Generate Scripts**:

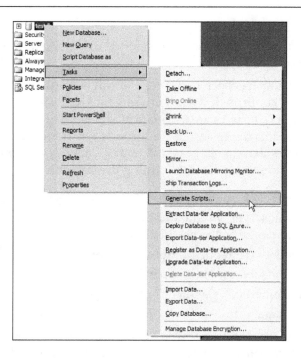

4. On the **Set Scripting Options** screen, click on **Advanced** to bring up the **Advanced Scripting Options** window. Then select the **Script for the database engine type** option, as shown below:

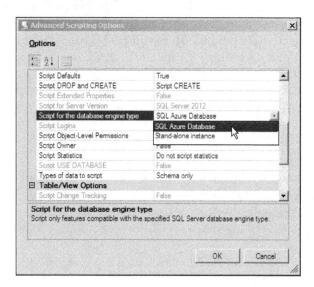

5. Complete the wizard to create the script file.

6. Connect to SQL Azure.

7. Run the script file you have just generated in order to create the objects on the SQL Azure instance.

At this point the schema has been migrated and can be verified on the SQL Azure instance. Once this is confirmed, we can migrate the data. This can be done using BCP, the bulk copy API, or with an automatically generated SSIS package. We will use the last option as it is the easiest of the three. It also has the advantage that it will first move those tables that do not have referential integrity dependencies on other tables, saving time and work when performing the transfer.

1. In SSMS, right click on the source database and select **Export Data**.

2. Select the local server and database as the source, then the SQL Azure server and database as the destination.

3. Select **Copy data from one or more tables or views**.

4. Select all of the tables in the source database.

5. Select **Run Immediately** and click on the **Finish** button.

6. Wait for the data to transfer to the SQL Azure database.

Open up the SQL Azure database and run a SELECT statement against one of the tables to check that the data has been transferred. It is as easy as that!

Public cloud costs

In this book, we will not go into precise figures as the charges are adjusted regularly, but costs are typically based on database size and bandwidth usage from the cloud service (traffic to the cloud is not billed). Further costs are incurred when moving data between different data centers, for instance, databases serving the US and European markets. Currently, costs can be as low as $5 per month for a 100MB database, and various free options exist under the MSDN subscription.

At the time of writing the latest offers for SQL Azure could be found at:

`www.microsoft.com/windowsazure/offers`.

There is a good explanatory video from Microsoft explaining how SQL Azure costs are calculated here:

`www.microsoft.com/en-us/showcase/details.`
`aspx?uuid=09aa4f10-333a-4c98-aed1-4cb300de63ec`.

Cloud service provider Cedexis publishes free reports about cloud services. They cover useful metrics such as performance and availability, load times and error rates. Their website can be found at:

`http://www.cedexis.com/country-reports/`.

The most attractive pricing option is the no commitment, consumption-based model, where you pay as you go (or as Microsoft call it, "Pay as you grow"). The advantage of this model is that there is no need to buy lots of hardware up front in anticipation of expected increases in business volume. This is what we term "ROI lag", when you put money up front, then hope you increase your sales in line with expectations, waiting for it to be paid off by the extra business that comes in over time.

However, you can purchase capacity up front and receive a discount if your sales volumes are growing predictably. This is what Microsoft calls the commitment model, where you pay to use the service for a fixed period of time at a lower cost.

Differences between SQL Azure and SQL Server Standard/Enterprise editions

There are two editions of SQL Azure. The Web Edition is for smaller databases up to 5GB in size, which often sit behind web applications, with pricing increments for each extra GB used. The Business Edition is aimed at applications such as CRM, customer support and HR systems, with databases ranging from 10 GB to 150 GB in size, with pricing increments in blocks of 10GB..

Using SQL Azure

As a developer, SQL Azure has minimal impact on the way you work, though you may need to perform a one-off re-write of some of your code. DBAs are affected to a greater degree, though it has the potential to reduce your workload in the long term. The best advice is to jump onboard as soon as you hear about migrations to SQL Azure, so that you can assess and advise what is technically feasible and what is not.

New skills

Fundamentally, no new skills need to be acquired as, with the possible exception of federations, most things that can be done in SQL Azure, can be done in SQL Server. We do need to learn a few things about moving data from SQL Server to SQL Azure, but this is very easy, as we have already seen. In general, it is best to think of SQL Azure as a limited subset of the main SQL Server product we are all familiar with.

 The full list of SQL Azure limitations can be found at:
`http://msdn.microsoft.com/en-us/library/windowsazure/ff394102`.

SQL Azure and the future of databases

Let us cut through the hype and marketing. Microsoft would love to have us all as hosted customers. So would Oracle and IBM. We in turn reduce capital expenditure and support costs and gain the advantages of scalability, whilst they gain complete control of the environment (which reduces their support costs) as well as gaining revenue. It all sounds straightforward and without a single problem encountered along the way. But, as we have discussed, that is not going to happen in the real world we inhabit, at least with some of the systems we support. The three main reasons are control, trust and regulation.

Control: If something goes wrong with a critical service we host ourselves, we have dedicated engineers on hand to fix it. There is a fundamental mistrust with third-party service providers, in that your account is one of many; if your critical system goes wrong in the cloud, it might be your business' highest priority to fix it, but it probably isn't theirs.

Trust: Unless you have physical access control over your data, you can never be totally certain that someone has not walked off with it. True, it shouldn't happen, but haven't we all set up email accounts that receive spam within 24 hours, or heard stories of personal data being sold to the highest bidder? If we have our own physical access control in place, we have taken a huge step towards preventing that problem. As soon as we entrust that to someone else, we lose control. It is similar to the concept of home working — it should happen in practice, but very few managers enjoy relinquishing control.

Regulation: Some jurisdictions state that personal data cannot be moved across borders. Data protection legislation enforces this and imposes heavy per-record fines on those who ignore it. Furthermore, there are restrictions such as the **International Traffic in Arms Regulations (ITAR)**. This protects highly sensitive US government data, where it can only be moved to or processed in a strictly defined set of trusted countries by trusted end users. It sounds unlikely that you would ever encounter this in a commercial environment, but the authors are aware of at least one publicly listed organisation outside of the USA where this has been subject to review and subsequent enforcement by the US State Department. Ignoring this kind of enforcement is usually subject to a prison sentence and exceptional fines.

 If you deal with US government data, read the following article describing the civil and criminal penalties for violation of the ITAR agreement: `http://www.cistec.or.jp/english/service/report/0802ITARarticleforCISTEC.pdf`.

In conclusion, we can reduce our server farm estate, or perhaps even migrate legacy applications to SQL Azure, as our hardware becomes redundant or out of warranty. But we must be aware of what is practical and possible to migrate, both technically and legally.

Finally, we must be aware of the one major feature we have not yet mentioned, which is not available with SQL Server, but is open to limited trial on SQL Azure — Hadoop.

Big data and Hadoop: horses for courses

Next, we are going to touch on subjects you may be unfamiliar with. Until now, the Hadoop big data platform has been an open source, Linux-based system. The good news is that soon it will be Windows-based, delivering an easier to understand and configure, and more reliable system. First, let us look at big data.

What is big data?

Think of three "V"s:

- **Velocity** is the speed at which data is being thrown at your database. Data feeds from places such as stock exchanges or some industrial processes overwhelm relational databases. Technologies such as **StreamInsight** are one answer, allowing us to filter out just the data we need. But sometimes we want to keep all of the data, perhaps for later processing, or maybe for reporting, analytics or data mining.

- **Volume** is the size of data being queried. Monitoring instruments, or web feeds from a very busy commercial site, may create so much data that it is not practical or required to break it down, process it and store it relationally. Nor may we need to, as perhaps we only require very simple reporting.

- **Variability** is perhaps the most intangible. Frequently, the need to store unstructured data is quoted as a big data platform advantage. In reality, most feeds conform to some protocol, even if it is CSV or XML and can be easily parsed. However, in a busy system, this parsing may not be practical in near-real time, so the ability to consume these feeds in a relatively raw, unstructured state can make sense.

The need for big data platforms

We need big data platforms such as Hadoop because of the overwhelming increase in the volume of corporate data we handle. Relational systems such as SQL Server, Oracle and DB2 were conceived to be high volume, small transaction systems, not to handle terabytes of streamed or unstructured data: it is not their strength. However, be aware that the cost of this new technology can be high, as it is not as simple to integrate into existing systems as its advocates suggest.

Due to its relative immaturity, there is not a rich tool set for moving data onto and off the platform, and the tools that do exist have their limitations. Porting data from Hadoop can mean transporting data files around for loading into your SQL Server tables using the SQL Server tool set. Getting data back onto the Hadoop platform can be slightly easier, as you just need to copy your data files into the appropriate directory on the **Hadoop Distributed File System (HDFS)** and tell **Hive** that it is there. But both processes lack automation, which obviously introduces latency.

When Microsoft ship Hadoop on the Windows platform, setup and integration may become easier and more efficient. But if you want the advantages that relational systems offer, do not go down the big data platform route. If you do not know what the advantages are, it is probably best to stop here and learn about why basic things like **ACID (Atomicity, Consistency, Isolation, Durability)** properties, transactions and relational theory are important before you get into hot water. We doubt most SQL Server people would fall into this trap, because you learn the importance of these things as a developer and DBA.

At present, most big data systems are *not* suited for use in an OLTP environment, which is where most data resides. They do not offer typical OLTP features and they present levels of latency that are simply unacceptable for most uses.

What they *are* suited to, is analytical reporting and data warehouse scenarios with overwhelming volumes of data (we are talking about 10TB plus per day and not 10GB).

The bottom line is this: just because Google, Facebook, or Twitter have a legitimate need for big data does not mean it is suitable for *your* business. Theirs are fundamentally different data needs, in very different businesses to those in which most of us work. Often the same results can be achieved more effectively with existing relational systems, with existing skill sets, sooner and at much lower expense. It can be done without the need for existing, experienced developers on a known, stable platform becoming complete novices on a new and less mature one. Think carefully about the alternatives before deciding to head down the big data route and *don't* get swept along with the hype.

Is SQL Server redundant?

SQL Server is far from redundant, in fact, quite the opposite. Similarly, Oracle, DB2 and Sybase will not be disappearing either. Cutting through the hype and ill-informed claims, it is important to realize that big data platforms exist for one purpose, relational systems for another. It is useful to think of big data platforms as a front end to the relational platform, one that can funnel data in from high volume, high velocity data streams, and perform basic analysis or processing on it before being brought into a relational environment. They are not a replacement for relational systems, and it is best to ignore ill-informed statements that claim they are. The next diagram illustrates where they sit architecturally in those rare scenarios where they are a requirement:

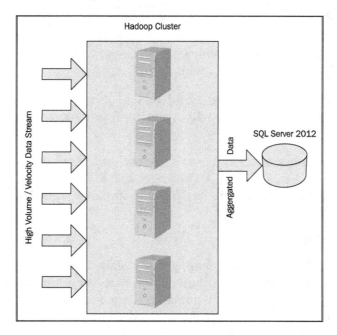

Given the rapid changes we are currently seeing in storage technology, relational engines have had a new lease of life breathed into them. Solid state (SSD) storage offers data retrieval speeds that could only have been dreamed of two years ago, with data read speeds in the 100,000s) **IOPS (Input/Outputs Per Second)** range. In comparison, a typical hard disk is capable of 150 to 200 IOPS. If anything, big data platforms have to prove that they are worthwhile for migrating certain functions, given what we can do at minimal cost and minimal disruption to business functions with new plug-and-play hardware. In addition, the **columnstore** feature of SQL Server 2012 means there are even more reasons to look at relational OLAP instead of going down the MOLAP or big data appliance route.

About Hadoop

Although it is a common preconception, **Hadoop** is not a database; Hadoop is a **Distributed File System (DFS),** which can be thought of as a software framework. It allows the manipulation of large amounts of data across one or more distributed and resilient nodes. It does this by running **MapReduce** functions against the data, which are typically written in a high-level programming language, such as Java. The same **MapReduce** algorithm is then run against different parts of the same data, with the data stored on multiple Hadoop nodes.

This does not mean that files are split up across multiple physical servers or devices as they are in a RAID array. Rather, multiple copies are stored, usually one copy on at least three servers. This has two major advantages—resilience and scalability. The former is an advantage because if one node of a Hadoop cluster goes down, the files it contains are available elsewhere. It is scalable because Hadoop can perform processing of a file on one server, whilst performing the same or different processing on the same or a different file, on a different server.

This massive, parallel capability has the advantage of being able to scale out very easily, so if you run out of capacity, you simply add more nodes to the Hadoop cluster.

Hadoop is not the only answer to these problems, but it is rapidly becoming accepted as one of the best and most mature; so much so, that Microsoft announced in 2011 that it will be porting Hadoop from its native environment, Linux, to Windows.

About Hive

When discussing Hive, we are not dealing with databases as we normally understand them, but rather as distributed data stores (or files if you like). A Hive database stores its data in structured directories, often as plaintext files such as CSV or tab delimited. The closest you will come to a **clustered primary index** is actually more equivalent to a partition - in fact it *is* a Hive partition, and you can only have one of them!

For example, if you have a Hive table that holds registration data, you can only have one partition in Hive. For this scenario, let's say it makes sense to partition on the registration date. On the Hive Distributed File System (HDFS), a likely setup is that there would be a directory with the same name as the table. In that directory would be a folder for each date (as this is the partition field) and in those folders would be one or more text files containing the data from that date in a uniformly structured format file, such as CSV. This is the reason you can only have one partition—the folder structure. But these things can change quite quickly in the open source world.

Whilst the above sounds reasonably unpalatable to anyone familiar with SQL Server, Hive does have an ANSI-92 SQL query processor which turns **Hive Query Language** (also known as **HiveQL** and **HQL**) into MapReduce jobs. In turn they are executed on the HDFS filesystem against the data files we have pulled from our data stream. It sounds complex, but the alternative is to write MapReduce jobs, which is analogous to handcoding **MDX** and not a preferable option.

Furthermore, it is worth noting that currently the command dictionary for Hive is not as complete as T-SQL. Notably, it is missing the negating logic commands. For instance, you can perform a UNION ALL but not a UNION. You can query using IN but not NOT IN. Furthermore you cannot just perform an INSERT into a hive table—you have to use INSERT OVERWRITE, obliterating any data that was already there... now ask yourself, do you really want to replace your relational platform with one that does this?

It is rather like working with SQL Server 6.5 after working with SQL Server 7 or better for the last 10 years! On the up-side, it forces you to think around certain problems, and you may well find yourself a better SQL programmer for the experience.

The following diagram displays how it all fits together. The Linux installation can be any version that supports Hadoop, though **Cloudera**'s VM, the one that we selected, uses **CentOS**. The Hadoop Distributed File System is spread across the data nodes with a copy of each data file on each data node.

 Cloudera's VM distribution of Hadoop can be found at: http://www. Cloudera.com/hadoop/.

This redundancy gives Hadoop its reliability and scalability. MapReduce jobs run on Hadoop, performing huge, parallel processing across the data nodes thereby giving Hadoop its speed. MapReduce jobs are difficult to write, so Hive sits on top of Hadoop/HDFS, converting ANSI-92 standard SQL to MapReduce code.

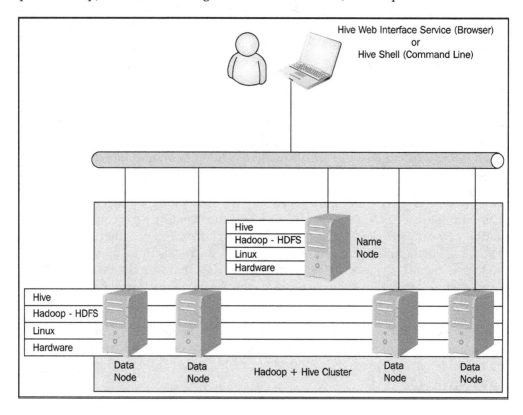

Differences in the Microsoft environment

Although nothing is definite until released, the major difference we will see is that Linux will be replaced by Windows. Any differences in the underlying Hadoop code will likely be hidden from view. The advantage from a DBA and developer perspective is that we should be able to address Hive directly using T-SQL, or at least an ANSI-92 standard subset of it. The ability to query and amend directly from SQL Server, perhaps using a linked server, would be a major bonus, but we have yet to see what tools Microsoft will provide us with to move data in and out of Hadoop. Given the Hive structure, SQL Server Integration Services (**SSIS**) may well be adapted and developments in the **Sqoop** connector (more on this later) may remove some of the pain. Obviously, you would expect Microsoft to take advantage of its current tool set where possible, when integrating the two.

Hadoop and OLTP

Implementing an OLTP system on Hadoop is a *really bad* idea because latency
is a major barrier to using Hadoop in any operation. Fault tolerance and scalable
analytics are the target, not response time. Nor is it appropriate for operations
that require transactional integrity, as the concept simply does not exist at present.

Getting started with Hadoop

To begin using Hadoop, you need four things: Hadoop, Hive, **VMWare Player** and
a method for moving data in and out of Hadoop. The first two are the most daunting
if you have a Microsoft background. However, and fortunately for us, the two main
Hadoop vendors, **Hortonworks** and **Cloudera**, are in stiff competition with each
other, and therefore simplifying the use of their products.

Until Hadoop becomes available on the Windows platform, we recommend you take
a look at Cloudera's Hadoop+Hive offering, called **Cloudera Demo VM**. This can be
downloaded from the Cloudera site and run as a virtual machine using the **VMWare
Player**, as shown in the following screenshot:

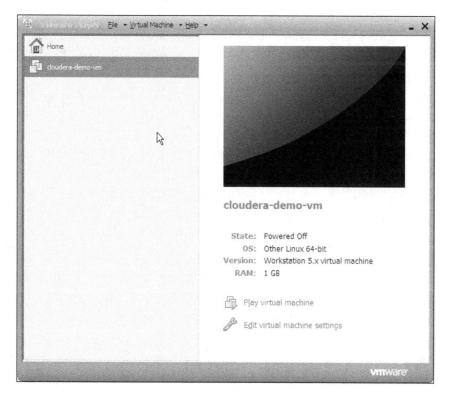

The Microsoft Hadoop/Sqoop connector

The next thing you need is a way to move data from SQL Server into Hadoop and back out again after processing. This is achieved by installing the Sqoop connector on the name node of the Hadoop cluster. **Sqoop** is a bi-directional, open source framework that facilitates data transfer between SQL Server tables and Hadoop in the form of either text or binary files. We have documented how we did this below, but hopefully, by the time you read this book, you will be able to use Hadoop on the Windows platform, which will be easier.

The SQL Server to Hadoop connector is a **Java Database Connectivity** (JDBC) connector driver that allows SQL Server and Hadoop to talk to each other through a framework known as Sqoop.

The installation procedure must take place on the Linux machine, and unfortunately can be a less than straightforward task. The following list is used for checking the installation.

- Check if Sqoop is already installed on the Linux installation. Open a command shell (terminal session) and type:

  ```
  sqoop version
  ```

  If it reports v1.3.0 or later versions, then you are fine (it should give this result, as it is shipped with Cloudera's Centos Linux release).

- Set environment variables.

  You will probably find that the environment variables the SQL Server-Hadoop Sqoop connector needs in order to work aren't set, so you need to perform this task.

  To set environment variables in Linux, start up a command shell (terminal session) and type the following:

  ```
  export SQOOP_HOME=/usr/lib/sqoop
  export SQOOP_CONF_DIR=/usr/lib/sqoop/conf
  ```

  `set` (to check that both environment variables have been set)

- Download the Microsoft JDBC driver (from www.microsoft.com/en-us/download/details.aspx?id=21599) onto the Linux machine.

  The SQL Server to Hadoop Connector needs JDBC to make it work, so unpack it from the command line using the following:

  ```
  cd Desktop
  tar -zxvf sqljdbc_3.0.1301.101_enu.tar.gz
  ```

The unzipped folder will appear on the desktop. Open the folder and then the ENU folder beneath it. You will need to copy the `sqljdbc4.jar` file, so open a terminal session:

Type: `cd /usr/lib/sqoop`

Type (on one line): `sudo cp /home/Cloudera/Desktop/sqljdbc_3.0/enu/sqljdbc4.jar`

    `sqljdbc4.jar`

- Download and install the SQL Server to Hadoop Connector.

 The SQL Server to Hadoop Data Connector can be found at: `www.microsoft.com/en-us/download/details.aspx?id=27584`.

To start using it, download and save it to the desktop on the Linux machine.

Next, open up a terminal session and type:

```
cd Desktop

tar -zxvf sqoop-sqlserver-1.0.tar.gz

cd sqoop-sqlserver-1.0

export MSSQL_CONNECTOR_HOME=/home/Cloudera/Desktop/sqoop-sqlserver-1.0

bash install.sh
```

If the installer says that it does not have permissions, run the following:

```
sudo bash install.sh
```

If it then states that the environment variables that were previously created are not set, just set them again and run `install.sh`. This happens because the environment variables are local to the particular terminal session in which they are created, and when `sudo bash` is invoked, a new session is created that cannot see the previously created environment variables.

Microsoft has a dedicated web page for setting up the Hadoop connector, but it is not comprehensive if you have never used Linux or Unix before:

```
http://www.microsoft.com/downloads/details.aspx?FamilyID=E579427E-
FFB6-49FE-98A3-C3435F8F742D&amp;displaylang=en&displaylang=en.
```

Notes on the Microsoft Hadoop/Sqoop connector

The Sqoop connector has been ported for both SQL Server and Oracle (ORAOOP), among others. However, both the SQL Server and Oracle connectors can prove problematical in operation. For instance, you can specify a query to extract a subset of data from SQL Server, but you cannot do this with Hive (you have to extract an entire table). This may mean an additional data preparation phase, where you prepare on Hive a table of just the data you are interested in, before pulling it into SQL Server with Sqoop. Sure, you can pull an entire table, but physical restrictions can make moving gigabytes of data a painfully slow process, which can be affected by network time outs, outages or transport limits. This pain is amplified if your OLTP and Hadoop platform are remote from each other. Even if they are on the same network, if you are moving hundreds of gigabytes of data around, you have to think how this will affect the rest of your network.

Remember that these technologies are in their infancy and as their use becomes more common, the lessons learned will percolate through to the products.

Summary

In this final chapter, we looked at using SQL Server in the cloud and why we would want to do this. We looked at big data, what is coming in the future from Microsoft and how it will come to broaden our skill sets as DBAs and developers. We cut through the marketing hype to discuss useful and objective, real-world advice about what these platforms can and cannot do, laying to rest the idea that they are soon to replace relational platforms.

A final word from the authors

We hope you have enjoyed reading our book and found the content useful! It was a labour of over ten month's effort between the two of us and nothing quite prepares you for writing something of even this modest size. If you have any requests for subjects you would like us to cover in the next edition, or wish to report any errors you have spotted, then please let us know.

Twitter: **@JonReade** and **@RachelClements**.

Index

mirroring 171
model
  multidimensional and data mining 80
  PowerPivot for SharePoint 80, 83
  previously installed model, determining
      86-90
  tabular 80, 81
msdb database 177
MS Hadoop/Sqoop connector 208-210
multidimensional and data mining model
  about 80
  database, creating 81
  installing 84, 85
Multidimensional Expressions. *See* MDX

N

New Data Quality Project button 164
New Knowledge Base button 152
New Query Edition Window 96
NT 183

O

Object Explorer pane 115
OFFSET 54-56
OLTP
  and Hadoop 207
operational data quality 145
OPEX 194
Options dialog box 24
Other Sources section 137
Output Data Preview grid 166

P

package
  comparing 130
  merging 130
  validating 127-129
package execution logs
  about 131
  basic logging, setting up 132
  logging results, viewing 133
package execution reports 133, 135
PackagePath property 140
PARSE 52, 53
Planning screen 13

PowerPivot for the SharePoint model
  about 83
  installing 85, 86
PowerPivot workbooks 83, 84
Power View
  about 100
  Data Alert 102
  tutorial 100
preprocessing 185
private cloud 196
public cloud 196

R

RDL files 101
redo 126
refId attribute 130
regulation 200
Report Builder
  about 102
  using 102
Reporting Services
  about 99
  deprecated features 99, 100
resources 142
Resource Usage reporting 90-94
Run button 184

S

SaaS 194
SAN 26
scalar functions. *See* string functions
security management
  about 35
  default schemas for groups 35
  SQL Server Audit enhancements 37
  user defined server roles 35, 36
Sequence 56-60
SequencingMode 190
Server Configuration screen 16
Server Roles node 35
Setup Support Rules screen 14
setup wizard 12
Shared Features 71
SharePoint Server 2010
  Power View 100, 101
Show all events checkbox 92

Simple Recovery mode 176
SMEs 146
software as a service. *See* SaaS
solid state disks (SSD) 8
spatial indexes 27
SPIDs 186
SQL Azure
  about 194
  limitations 199
  migrating to, business reasons 194
SQL Server
  administration 23
  challenges 193
  redundancy 203
SQL Server 2008 R2 99
SQL Server 2012
  about 7
  Analysis Services 79
  editions 7, 8
  evaluating 11
  installation process, navigating 12-22
  retailing 12
SQL Server Audit enhancements 37
SQL Server Data Quality Services. *See* DQS
SQL Server Data Tools. *See* SSDT
SQL Server Data Tools checkbox 71
SQL Server Development Settings 76
SQL Server Distributed Replay
      Client service 187
 SQL Server Distributed Replay
      Controller service 186
SQL Server Integration Services. *See* SSIS
SQL Server Management Studio. *See* SSMS
SQL Server Profiler
  about 184
  using 90
Sqoop 208
Sqoop connector 206
SSDT
  about 69, 81, 119
  database projects 70
  debugging 71
  installing new project, creating 72, 73
  installing 71
  installing, without Visual Studio 2010
      pre-installed 71

installing, with Visual Studio 2010
      pre-installed 71
  IntelliSense 70
  version connection support 70
SSIS 105, 206
SSIS 2012
  functions 118
ssis_admin role
  about 108
  users access, giving to integration services
      109-114
SSIS Control Flow tab 137
SSISDB 106, 107
SSMS 70, 133
Standard Edition 10
Start Visual Studio button 73
status codes
  colour coded 130
  indicator 131
STBuffer functions 27
STDistance functions 27
Storage Area Network. *See* SAN
StreamInsight 201
StressScaleGranularity 190
string functions
  about 41
  CONCAT() 42, 43
  FORMAT() 43
String store constraint
  about 95
  scalable string storage, using 95, 96
StringStoresCompatibilityLevel property
      95
subject matter experts. *See* SMEs
sys.dm_db_mirroring_auto_page_repair 177
sys.dm_hadr_auto_page_repair 177

T

tabular model
  about 81
  database 81
  database, creating 83
  installing 84, 85
  xVelocity engine mode 82
tabular model database
  creating 82

Thank you for buying
What's new in SQL Server 2012

About Packt Publishing

Packt, pronounced 'packed', published its first book "Mastering phpMyAdmin for Effective MySQL Management" in April 2004 and subsequently continued to specialize in publishing highly focused books on specific technologies and solutions.

Our books and publications share the experiences of your fellow IT professionals in adapting and customizing today's systems, applications, and frameworks. Our solution based books give you the knowledge and power to customize the software and technologies you're using to get the job done. Packt books are more specific and less general than the IT books you have seen in the past. Our unique business model allows us to bring you more focused information, giving you more of what you need to know, and less of what you don't.

Packt is a modern, yet unique publishing company, which focuses on producing quality, cutting-edge books for communities of developers, administrators, and newbies alike. For more information, please visit our website: www.packtpub.com.

About Packt Enterprise

In 2010, Packt launched two new brands, Packt Enterprise and Packt Open Source, in order to continue its focus on specialization. This book is part of the Packt Enterprise brand, home to books published on enterprise software – software created by major vendors, including (but not limited to) IBM, Microsoft and Oracle, often for use in other corporations. Its titles will offer information relevant to a range of users of this software, including administrators, developers, architects, and end users.

Writing for Packt

We welcome all inquiries from people who are interested in authoring. Book proposals should be sent to author@packtpub.com. If your book idea is still at an early stage and you would like to discuss it first before writing a formal book proposal, contact us; one of our commissioning editors will get in touch with you.

We're not just looking for published authors; if you have strong technical skills but no writing experience, our experienced editors can help you develop a writing career, or simply get some additional reward for your expertise.

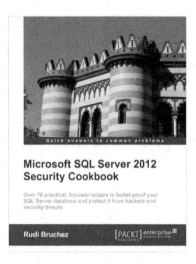

Microsoft SQL Server 2012

Security Cookbook

**Microsoft SQL Server 2012
Security Cookbook**

ISBN: 978-1-84968-588-7   Paperback: 350 pages

Over 70 practical, focused recipes to bullet-proof your
SQL Server database and protect it from hackers and
security threats

Over 70 practical, focused recipes to bullet-proof your
SQL Server database and protect it from hackers and
security threats

Rudi Bruchez

1. Practical, focused recipes for securing your
    SQL Server databse

2. Master the latest techniques for data and
    code encryption, user authentication and
    authorization, protection against brute force
    attacks, denial-of-service attacks, and SQL
    Injection, and more

3. A learn-by-example recipe-based approach
    that focuses on key concepts to provide the
    foundation to solve real world problems

**SQL Server 2012 with PowerShell
V3 Cookbook**

**SQL Server 2012 with
PowerShell V3 Cookbook**

ISBN: 978-1-84968-646-4   Paperback: 635 pages

Increase your productivity as a DBA, developer, or IT
Pro, by using PowerShell with SQL Server to simplify
database management and automate repetitive,
mundane tasks.

Increase your productivity as a DBA, developer, or IT Pro,
by using PowerShell with SQL Server to simplify database
management and automate repetitive, mundane tasks.

Donabel Santos

1. Provides over a hundred practical recipes that
    utilize PowerShell to automate, integrate and
    simplify SQL Server tasks

2. Offers easy to follow, step-by-step guide
    to getting the most out of SQL Server
    and PowerShell

3. Covers numerous guidelines, tips, and
    explanations on how and when to use
    PowerShell cmdlets, WMI, SMO, .NET
    classes or other components

Please check **www.PacktPub.com** for information on our titles

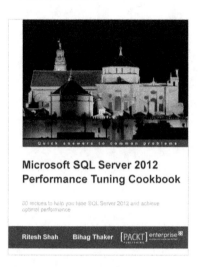

Microsoft SQL Server 2012 Performance Tuning Cookbook

ISBN: 978-1-84968-574-0   Paperback: 478 pages

80 recipes to help you tune SQL Server 2012 and achieve optimal performance

1. Learn about the performance tuning needs for SQL Server 2012 with this book and ebook

2. Diagnose problems when they arise and employ tricks to prevent them

3. Explore various aspects that affect performance by following the clear recipes

**Microsoft SQL Server 2012
Performance Tuning Cookbook**

80 recipes to help you tune SQL Server 2012 and achieve optimal performance

Ritesh Shah   Bihag Thaker

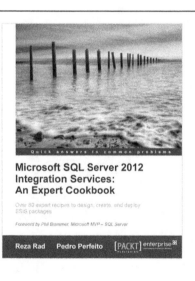

Microsoft SQL Server 2012 Integration Services: An Expert Cookbook

ISBN: 978-1-84968-524-5   Paperback: 564 pages

Over 80 expert recipes to design, create, and deploy SSIS packages

1. Full of illustrations, diagrams, and tips with clear step-by-step instructions and real time examples

2. Master all transformations in SSIS and their usages with real-world scenarios

3. Learn to make SSIS packages re-startable and robust; and work with transactions

4. Get hold of data cleansing and fuzzy operations in SSIS

**Microsoft SQL Server 2012
Integration Services:
An Expert Cookbook**

Over 80 expert recipes to design, create, and deploy SSIS packages

Foreword by Phil Brammer, Microsoft MVP – SQL Server

Reza Rad   Pedro Perfeito

Please check **www.PacktPub.com** for information on our titles

www.ingramcontent.com/pod-product-compliance
Lightning Source LLC
LaVergne TN
LVHW062313060326
832902LV00013B/2198

* 9 7 8 1 8 4 9 6 8 7 3 4 8 *